The Flipside of Godspeak

The Flipside of Godspeak:
Theism as Constructed Reality

John F. Crosby

Resource *Publications*

An imprint of Wipf and Stock Publishers
199 West 8th Avenue • Eugene, OR 97401

THE FLIPSIDE OF GODSPEAK
Theism as Constructed Reality

Copyright © 2006 John F. Crosby. All rights reserved. Except for brief quotations in critical publications or reviews, no part of this book may be reproduced in any manner without prior written permission from the publisher. Write: Permissions, Wipf & Stock, 199 W. 8th Ave., Eugene, OR 97401.

ISBN 10: 1-59752-849-8
ISBN 13: 978-1-59752-849-8

Manufactured in the U.S.A.

For those who know they don't know.

I deeply appreciate those who have given me constructive feedback at different stages along the way. Thanks to Janet Meacham for her encouragement and editing of the initial draft and to Leora Baude for her deft hand in copyediting the final product.

"The religious intolerance so characteristic of Western religions . . . has led to a new form of idolatry. an image of god, not in wood and stone but in words, is erected so that people worship at this shrine."

> Erich Fromm, *Psychoanalysis and Religion*, 1950

"The idea that there is one people in possession of the truth, one answer to the world's ills, or one solution to humanity's needs has done untold harm throughout history."

> Kofi Annan, in his speech receiving the 2001 Nobel Peace Prize.

"If God did not exist, it would be necessary to invent him."

> Voltaire, 1694–1778

"The essential functions of the mind consist in understanding and in inventing, in other words, in building up structures by structuring reality."

> Jean Piaget, *Psychologie et Pedagogie*, 1969

CONTENTS

Other books by John F. Crosby
Introduction: Entering the Constructivist Arena / 1
Chapter One *Constructivism I: How We Create Reality* / 9
Chapter Two *Constructivism II: How We Learn* / 19
Chapter Three *The Quest for Truth* / 27
Chapter Four *Is There Really God? Faith Versus Knowledge* / 39
Chapter Five *The Anatomy of Theistic Belief* / 49
Chapter Six *Can There Be Morality without God?*
I: Authority in Ethics / 61
Chapter Seven *Can There Be Morality without God?*
II: An Ethic of Well-Being / 67
Chapter Eight *The Quest for Meaning and Purpose in Life* / 77

Afterword / 87
Appendix I *Confession of an Apostate* / 91
Appendix II *The Flipside of Godspeak for Agnostics and Non-Theists* / 105
Glossary / 111
Bibliography / 117

Other books by John F. Crosby

Witness for Christ. Westminster Press, 1965.

From Religion to Grace: The Doctrine of Justification by Grace Through Faith. Abingdon Press, 1967.

Illusion and Disillusion: The Self in Love and Marriage. Wadsworth Publishing Company, 1973, 1976, 1985, 1991.

Choice and Challenge: Contemporary Readings in Marriage. (Ed. with Carl Williams) William C. Brown Company, 1974, 1979.

Sexual Autonomy: Toward a Humanistic Ethic. Charles C. Thomas, 1981.

Reply to Myth: Perspectives on Intimacy. (Ed.) John Wiley & Sons, 1985.

When One Wants Out and the Other Doesn't: Doing Therapy With Polarized Couples. (Ed.) Brunner/Mazel, 1989.

Grounds For Marriage: If Only I Had Known. AuthorHouse, 2005.

Introduction

Entering the Constructivist Arena

I AM AN apostate. I am no longer a theist. Nor am I a deist.[1] I am a non-theist.[2] I no longer subscribe to a notion of transcendent force or being beyond this world or to an immanent force personally active in the affairs of humankind. I am an agnostic, because I claim to have absolutely no knowledge of any force or being that cannot be validated and verified via scientific methodology. I am also a humanist, an evolutionist, and an existentialist. These three terms translate into my belief that human existence is a given without any reference to the supernatural.

Judaism, Christianity, and Islam hold both to transcendence and immanence, be it in Yahweh, God, or Allah. In the name of Yahweh, God, and Allah, humankind continues to wage war with increasingly lethal weapons of mass destruction, to oppress and enslave women, to oppress and enslave children, and to rape and squander the environment and the natural resources of the planet. In the name of Yahweh, God, and Allah, the greatest social issues and problems facing humankind remain not only unsolved, but tragically ignored by those political and religious leaders who are in a position to promote meaningful change. These issues include world overpopulation, poverty in the Third World, treatment of females

---

[1] A *theist* is usually considered to believe in a supreme being who is both transcendent and immanent, i.e., both above the universe and present and active within the affairs of humankind. A *deist* holds that a supreme being or creative force is the uncaused prime cause of all creation. Deists also adhere to the argument from design, i.e., that the design and dynamic forces of the universe point to a supreme "designer" or eternal mind that underlies and sustains the entire operation but is not involved in the affairs of humankind.

[2] The term *non-theist* derives from the Latin *non*, which means no, none, or simply negative. The term *atheist* derives from the Greek *a*, which means without, or simply negative. While these terms literally mean the same thing Western society attaches less social stigma to the Latin version, *non-theist*. A negative or weak atheist says: "I do not believe in God." A positive or strong atheist says: "I believe there is no God."

as second-class citizens and/or chattel, lack of procreative health for both mothers and neonates, torture and extraordinary rendition, pollution of the environment and its resources, and total failure in energy conservation. Each of these religions, too often in league with the political establishment, clings to dogma asserting the will and purpose of its God-Author while at the same time teaching and proclaiming with near-hatred the inferiority of those who differ in worldview, be they homosexuals, pro-choicers, pacifists, or liberals of all descriptions.

Within Christianity there is a living pope, who claims infallibility in all ex-cathedra pronouncements, and a paper pope, consisting of scripture that is hailed by the faithful as being both without error and to be taken as literal truth in the most minor detail. Islam also has a paper pope, the Koran. Within Islam we find even greater enthusiasm for the subjugation of women and an apologia for the fighting of a holy war of terrorism.

All of the above exists in our American culture, which inherited the wisdom of such great Western philosophers as Socrates, Descartes, Spinoza, Locke, Berkeley, Hume, and Kant, to name only a few. We live in a society whose media, including television and motion pictures, and political and patriotic rhetoric pander to the taste and preferences of a general public with an eighth-grade reading level. At most recent glance, the public thirst for violence appears to be at a third- or fourth-grade level.

Theism and its increasingly popular godspeak are a major part of the problem facing the world today. Godspeak is the easy reference to deity and the will of deity, ranging from attributing natural and human events to God to the familiar praising of God and blessing of God, including the invoking of God's blessing upon certain groups of humans. Godspeak is the sum total of speaking in familiar and intimate terms about the purposes of God and the will of God.

The fusion of popular godspeak with political rhetoric proclaiming the kingdom of God in alliance with the alleged supremacy of capitalism and capitalistic democracy has led to a nationalistic theology characterized by pietism and patriotism. This national religion has reached such an extreme expression that criticism of political policy and an open questioning of religious dogma is labeled unpatriotic at best and treasonous at worst. Devotees of the nationalized God of Western capitalism look upon atheists, agnostics, and humanists as both unpatriotic and blasphemous.

My deep distrust and disdain for this nationalized patriotic piety and a renewed awareness of how and why believers and devotees allow it to guide and direct their thought processes led me to delve more deeply into claims concerning the authority of the biblical scriptures, the selection of

Introduction

the canon, and the orthodoxy that grew out of the councils of the fourth century, especially the Council of Nicea in 325 CE.[3] What leads people to embrace the rightest theologies and the conservative agendas that are today so pervasive in our society? What leads people to eschew sound biblical scholarship in favor of acceptance of a wooden literalism and belief in the inerrancy of scripture? The further I traveled into the world of constructivist theory, the more committed I became to the task of understanding theistic theologies in the light of the basic epistemological question, how do we know what we believe we know?

The thoughts contained in *The Flipside of Godspeak* are not necessarily new, nor are they unique. They are, however, foreign to the aforementioned pietistic and patriotic devotees of the neo-cons, the religious conservatives, the religious far right, and the rapturists.

In writing *The Flipside of Godspeak*, I present myself as an apostate, because I was once a devout Christian believer. Looking back, I regret that I ever endorsed the basic tenets of the Christian faith. The most significant exception to this is my acceptance of what we can know of the historical Jesus. Looking back, I'm now certain that I believed in the Christian message, the *kerygma*, for psycho-emotional reasons, even though I always considered myself a liberal and free-thinking Presbyterian. As my thinking evolved, I have grown to the point that I no longer need whatever meaning, peace, and emotional security the Christian message ever held for me.

In the pages that follow, I shall attempt to take the reader with me as I retrace my steps on my theological journey that has its roots in philosophy and psychology. Specifically, this volume is an application of psychological and philosophical constructivism to the question of the existence of God.[4] A recent dictionary definition of a *construct* is something constructed by the mind.[5] "For constructivists, all communication and all understanding are a matter of interpretive construction on the part of the experiencing subject."[6] Constructivism refers to the filtering and processing of all sen-

---

[3] "The third period (of the establishment of the canon) begins in 325 and is marked by authoritative pronouncements, first by bishops of provincial churches and later by councils or synods. In 367 Athanasius put forth a list of 27 N.T. books, which corresponds to the present canon. At the synods of Hippo Regius (393) and Carthage (397, 419), our N.T. of 27 books was accepted." Henry Snyder Gehman, *The New Westminster Dictionary of the Bible* (Philadelphia: Westminster Press, 1970.) 146.

[4] Throughout the entire book I will capitalize the word *God* when it is used in a traditional sense to denote a single, omniscient and omnipotent deity, both immanent and transcendent.

[5] *Merriam-Webster's Collegiate Dictionary*, Eleventh Edition, 2003.

[6] Ernst von Glasersfeld, "An Introduction to Radical Constructivism" in *The Invented*

sory and mental images. Constructivism posits that "an organism is never able to recognize, depict, or mirror reality, and that it can only construct a 'model that fits.'"[7] In short, we do not know reality directly. All we can do is take in the data from outside ourselves and process it through our mind. In this process we form an internal mental image of what we think reality is.

I shall attempt to challenge the reader to see the dogmas and myths of revealed religious faith, including belief in a personal deity, as constructs of the human mind.[8] These beliefs are the result of early indoctrination, education, and socialization. I do not question or doubt that the Bible and other sacred literature, such as the Koran, the Vedas, and the Tao Te Ching, will always remain repositories of ancient wisdom. However, having said this, I must emphasize that there is no authority other than one's own human mind that has the power to bind the conscience and will of an individual, unless a person chooses to cede this authority to a force or power outside the self.

In my transition from Presbyterian cleric to constructivist, I have learned from many respected writers and thinkers, including philosophers and therapists, physicists and logicians. In my last two years as a minister, I immersed myself in the writings of Erich Fromm, Rollo May, Karen Horney, and Viktor Frankl. To this day I count those four as my primary life teachers. Much of what I have included in this small volume is a reflection of an attitude and viewpoint about life that I learned from them. Additionally, I grew to appreciate Sigmund Freud's *The Future of An Illusion*. I also administered to myself a strong dose of Herman Hesse and a modest dose of Kierkegaard, Nietzsche, Sartre, Kafka, and Camus.

A new world opened to me when I was doing my doctoral work at Syracuse and first discovered the wisdom and research of Jean Piaget, a ma-

---

Reality (New York: W.W. Norton & Company, 1984) 17-40.

[7] Fritz B. Simon et al., *The Language of Family Therapy: A Systemic Vocabulary and Sourcebook* (New York: Family Process Press, 1985) 67.

[8] The distinction between *natural* theology and *revealed* theology is extremely important. Natural theology is an appeal to the senses and the mind based on the wonder and experience of the macro universe and the micro universe. Natural theology appeals to human reason, whereby a person might base his/her faith on the world of natural phenomena. Basically, it is an argument from design, i.e., we observe the design of the natural order and we infer that some force has performed the role of designer. Revealed (based on the Latin word *revelare*, to uncover,) theology is based on the belief that a theistic force (God, Yahweh, Allah) has revealed itself to humankind in some manner. Buddhism, Hinduism,and Confucianism, among many others, are examples of non-theistic religions. Christianity, Judaism, and Islam are prime examples of revealed religions, although many liberal devotees of Christianity base their theistic beliefs on natural rather than revealed theology. Please see Appendix I for a more complete treatment of natural and revealed theology.

jor force in understanding the basic assumptions of constructivism. New vistas continued to open up as I took seriously the writings of Richard Dawkins,[9] Carl Sagan, and Ernest Becker.[10] In the 1970s and '80s I became increasingly immersed in family systems theory. My ongoing work as a professor of family studies and as a marriage/family therapist brought me face to face with the basic principles of systems theory and the related thought of constructivism. By the late 1980s, constructivism became the most salient influence on my thinking as I continued to struggle with the great questions of human existence, including the question of the existence of God.

I was strongly influenced by Paul Watzlawick, who constantly reminded me that in politics, international relations, theology, and family therapy, the solution frequently becomes the problem.[11] In terms of post 9/11 foreign policy and in the conduct of America's war on terrorism and the shameful Iraq experience, the solutions have compounded the problem. This is because attempted solutions such as preemptive strikes and invasions, increased arms production, and foreign policy based on America's presumptive right to impose its will around the globe (the Pax Americana) have done nothing but make the problem worse. This has happened to such an extent that America has lost the respect not only of its time-honored allies, but also of benign adversaries and Third World nations.

I began to apply the principles and insights of family systems theory and constructivism to issues and problems of both a political and theological nature. Murray Bowen's eighth premise of his family theory, the principle of societal regression, holds that societies go through similar processes as families in coping with anxiety and stress, i.e., the greater the threat to the balance of the family, the more emotional and irrational the consequent reaction.[12] I found Bowen's application of family systems theory to the issues and problems of societies a refreshing analysis of modern-day political efforts to solve the pressing issues facing the nations of the world, especially Westernized industrial nations.

---

[9] Dawkins, Richard, *The Selfish Gene* (New York: Oxford University Press, 1976); *The Blind Watchmaker* (New York: W. W. Norton, 1986).

[10] Sagan, Carl, *The Demon-Haunted World* (New York: Ballantine, 1996). Becker, Ernest, *The Denial of Death* (New York: The Free Press, 1973).

[11] Paul Watzlawick, *The Invented Reality* (New York: W. W. Norton, 1984); *Ultra Solutions* (New York: W.W. Norton, 1988). Gerald R. Weeks and Luciano L'Abate, *Paradoxical Psychotherapy* (New York: Bruner/Mazel, 1982)

[12] Murray Bowen, *Family Therapy In Clinical Practice* (New York: Jason Aronson, 1978). See Chapter 16, "Theory in the Practice of Psychotherapy."

THE FLIPSIDE OF GODSPEAK

I then challenged my own thought processes by asking the question: What would it look like if we applied the principles and premises of constructivism to theological and ontological issues? For starters, these issues include the entire range of beliefs about the nature of God, the condition of humankind, the foundation of ethics, the meaning of death, and the meaning of life.

Constructivism became my paradigm of choice in seeking to understand how we think and why we believe the things we do. In the first four decades of my life, I nurtured a mental construct in my mind that I called God. In my sixth decade, a new construct took root in my mind, and it led me to question theism to the point where I was able to see that it was simply *my wish-dream of how I wanted life to be*. I began to see how the God-solution to life's mysteries was a major contributor to the problems of international relations, peace among nations, and the ongoing struggle to give meaning to one's own existence.

I am setting these thoughts down in writing because I dare not wait any longer in the hope of availing myself of additional experience, knowledge, and wisdom. I am at that point in life wherein my window of opportunity may begin to decrease at an alarming rate. In the interest of accuracy, clarity, judgment, and organization, I do not wish to postpone this endeavor any longer. I will not permit myself to go to my death having remained silent about these matters. I invite you to think with me and share my reasoning and my logic. Let us embark on a journey into the tenets and ideas inherent in constructivism and then follow the logic of its implications into the questions of reality, theism, truth, ethics, and the meaning of human existence. For some readers this journey will be anxiety-producing because it will challenge traditional beliefs and traditional values. I hope that for most readers it will also be a confirming and validating experience that will serve as a springboard into further exploration and discovery in the ongoing and never-ending quest for truth.

Chapters One and Two plunge into the key theme of this book. *Constructivism* is not a panacea, nor is it an intellectual fad, here today and gone tomorrow. At the center of constructivism is the belief that the human mind, acting on past experience and continuous information from the senses and the processing of mental data, constructs its own images and ideas of reality. By implication, this means that our concepts of God, our images of God, are the product of the operations of our mind. We learn to construct what we cannot see and call it faith. We learn to create what we most wish to be true and call it reality. Then we learn to believe in what we have constructed. We learn to cast ourselves upon the very image of our mental construct in the faith that we shall find completion and fulfillment both in this life and in an afterlife. In this process we trust the alleged authority of would-be experts who point us to a supreme authority.

In the chapters that follow I shall attempt to make sense of human existence using the constructivist paradigm rather than the traditional theistic paradigm. The end result will place us in a world wherein we alone are the architects of our own existence, and we alone are responsible for the meaning and purpose that we give to our life and our journey though it.

Chapter One

Constructivism I: How We Create Reality

Jamie Nails, a Miami Dolphins offensive lineman who played in Buffalo for four seasons (for the Buffalo Bills professional football team) said the weather was mostly in the mind. "When Buffalo comes to Miami, it feels like 100 degrees to them and 70 to us, he said. "When we come up here, it feels 20 below to us, and 30 to them. It's all in the mind."[1]

"How do we know what we believe we know?"[2] This simple question has kept philosophers, mathematicians, and logicians busy since pre-Socratic times. According to Paul Watzlawick, the question essentially involves three areas of inquiry: (1) *What* we believe has to do with our understanding of the so-called real world, the way things really are. Most people believe that common sense is a trustworthy avenue to knowledge about objective reality. The attempt to discover and define objective reality is a derivative of metaphysics. It has to do with the nature of being, often referred to as ontology. (2) *How* we know has to do with epistemology, the study of how we come about knowing. Do we know what we think we know because of intuition? Or do we know because of firsthand experience? Or do we know because of scientific research? Or do we know because of some kind of revelation? (3) The *believe* part of the statement is usually referred to as constructivism, having its roots in thinkers such as Giambattista Vico, Immanuel Kant, David Hume, and Jean Piaget. Constructivism is the central theme of both this chapter and the next.

---

[1] *The New York Times*, Monday, December 2, 2002, the day after Miami lost to Buffalo in Buffalo amidst freezing temperatures and driving snow squalls.
[2] Paul Watzlawick, *The Invented Reality: Contributions to Constructivism.* (New York: W.W. Norton, 1984) 9–11.

THE FLIPSIDE OF GODSPEAK

Paul Watzlawick, a pioneer in the application of constructivism to human behavior, favors the terms *invention* or *invented reality* in order to indicate that reality is an invention of the mind and its processes as we seek to understand the world outside ourselves. Watzlawick further suggests the term *reality research* as being a more accurate and precise descriptor of the endeavor to invent, create, or construct reality.[3] I prefer the term *created reality*.[4] I dismiss the term *perception* or *perceived reality* because it conveys a sense of being a weak or watered down mental process.

What we know is always the partial result of how we came to know it. Watzlawick says, "If *what* we know depends on *how* we came to know it, then our view of reality is no longer a true image of what is the case outside ourselves, but is inevitably determined also by the processes through which we arrived at this view."[5] Betty Caldwell, a noted professor of child development under whom I studied at Syracuse University, frequently reminded me that there are no such things as facts apart from the methods by which these facts are obtained. By the same token, when we engage in discussion, debate, and dialogue, common sense dictates that if we grant the method, we can't lose. This is to say that once we grant the validity of the method of ascertaining the alleged facts, there is a certain presumption of logic in the process of drawing a conclusion from these facts. What we know is therefore always the product of how we come to know it. While we may believe that an object of any description is real, the reality of that object depends on our knowledge of that object. Reality is a *construct* of our mind, and were it not for our mental capacity to organize data about the object via our senses and our mental processes, we would not have knowledge of the alleged object.

---

[3] Ibid.

[4] From Andrew M. Colman, *Oxford Dictionary of Psychology* (Oxford University Press: Oxford, 2001): "Constructivism: A doctrine according to which perceptions, memories, and other complex mental structures are actively assembled or built by the mind, rather than being passively acquired. The idea was introduced in 1932 by the English psychologist Sir Frederic Charles Bartlett (1886–1969) to explain phenomena that he observed in his study of memory . . . Radical constructivism, deriving from writings in the 1950s of the Swiss psychologist Jean Piaget (1896–1980), is based on the assumption that children construct mental structures by observing the effects of their own actions on the environment."

[5] Watzlawick, *Invented Reality*, 9.

Objectivity and Subjectivity — The Observer and the Observed

Before we proceed further, let us distinguish constructivism from a philosophical school of thought known as solipsism. *Solipsism is the belief that all reality is in the mind and that there is no reality outside the mind.* Solipsism not only claims that reality is unknowable apart from the perceiving mind: it goes further, by claiming that reality is solely in the mind and never outside it.

Contrary to solipsism, constructivists do not claim there is no objective reality. They simply claim that whatever is called objective reality is unknowable apart from the processes of the human mind and the central nervous system.[6] Constructivists claim that what a person believes about the world outside the self (objects, phenomena, events, happenings, the universe, the galaxies, microcosoms, macrocosoms, history, geography, mathematics, physics, metaphysics, and theology) is a person's reality. Constructivism has to do with how we create and experience the world outside of ourselves. This is also known as second-order cybernetics.[7] The outside or objective world is there, but it can never be isolated from the subjective self who observes it. In this sense there is no such thing as purely objective analysis or purely objective reasoning. The observer always becomes a part of what is observed, be it an author who writes a book, a person who writes a letter, an experiment wherein the principal investigator claims the scientific method of objectivity, a historian writing history, or even a mathematician doing an advanced calculus.[8]

As much as a pollster may protest that he/she is being objective in the writing of questions to which a sample of the population will be asked to respond, there is a great deal of subjectivity in the way the question is phrased. What is not said may be more important that what is said. What is asked for may be material that will tend to establish the purpose of the ques-

---

[6] von Forrester, Heinz, "On Constructing a Reality," in *The Invented Reality*, ed. Paul Watzlawick (New York:W.W. Norton, 1984) 41–61.

[7] By way of contrast and comparison, first order cybernetics has to do with so-called black box or input-output interventions such as the thermostat and other self-regulating systems wherein the one who is in control calibrates the system in such a manner that the system will function without ongoing intervention. See Bradford P. Keeney, *Aesthetics of Change* (New York: The Guilford Press, 1983) 61–109.

[8] For an analysis and discussion of the role of the mathematician in the discipline of mathematics, see Gabriel Stolzenberg, "Can an Inquiry into the Foundations of Mathematics Tell Us Anything Interesting About Mind?" in Paul Watzlawick, *The Invented Reality* (New York: W.W. Norton, 1984) 257–308.

tioner, especially if the pollster is hired by a Democrat, a Republican, or any other political party member. I recently read an article by a syndicated columnist confessing that he did not vote in the Congressional elections. He claimed that to vote would have compromised his own objectivity and that he was much more likely to be free of bias if he refused to vote. Of course, to be consistent, this writer would have to void his mind of all involvement in any and every issue he chose to write about. The resulting product would be a miracle of literary fortitude. The observer (writer, teacher, historian, therapist, physician, mechanic, repairman) inevitably becomes a part of (involved in, identified with, linked with) what is observed.

Likewise, when you say to your friend, "My, wasn't that some speech (or lecture, or performance, or movie, or play, or football game)?" there is no question that you are asking for agreement with your own feelings about the matter. The questioner is subjectively involved in the question such that the answer is probably going to be in the affirmative.

Some stock brokerage houses charge their clients an annual fee rather than the customary broker percentage of every given stock purchase or sale. This way the brokerage firm can advertise that their brokers are absolutely objective because they are free of the profit motive. They are also (purportedly) not influenced by their own opinions and preferences. Hence, the brokers enjoy, so the line goes, a much greater degree of objectivity and freedom in their role as consultants. Supposedly the broker will be purely objective within a profession that is highly subjective. This, of course, is an exercise in self-delusion, because there is no possible way a stockbroker can be completely objective. Not even a computer can be completely objective, for the simple reason that the output of the computer is completely dependent on the instructions that have been programmed into the computer via the software, which in turn tells the computer what to do.

In the scientific world of research, a double-blind design is one of the most favored types of studies. In a double-blind design, the experimental subject does not know which experimental category he/she has been placed in, nor do the researchers know which experimental category the subjects have been placed in. This process would seem to eliminate observer bias. While this is undoubtedly a time-honored method for constructing a research design, there is still the often hidden bias of the hypothesis to be tested. Again, how the hypothesis is worded is never completely free of subjective contamination. In short, the observer frequently sees exactly what he/she *expects* to see.

Believing Is Seeing

Believing is seeing! We have all heard the direct opposite of this, that seeing is believing, and it often is. But believing is also seeing. We often see exactly what we expect to see. We form an unconscious image of what we are certain will be the results, and then we proceed to confirm our belief by selecting out contrary information. *The eye will always tend to see what the mind expects.* If it were not so, there would be no such thing as an illusionist. The illusionist is master at getting the observer to focus on the obvious so that he/she can control the hidden variables. When absolute attention is being paid to the object upon which the illusionist focuses your attention, there is ample opportunity for the illusionist to enact his/her own agenda in such a manner that no one sees or catches on to what the illusionist is really doing.

What is the basis of astrology? What is the basis of palm reading? How do tarot cards work? What ploy does a psychic use to build a client's belief? What is the basis of faith healing? Are there really aliens and extra terrestrials? Could there really be ghosts and haunted houses? Is there really such a thing as a Voodoo curse? What is the basis for the belief among many within our society that the best antidote or prescription for healing is a positive attitude? Why do some experts claim that laughter is the best medicine? What advantage does the hopeful optimist have over the dreary pessimist?

The most well-known example of believing-leading-to-seeing are the experiments wherein schoolteachers are told at the beginning of a term that certain students are low achievers or troublemakers. The same teachers are also told that certain other of their new students are high achievers or ultra-teachable. To no one's surprise, the results always seem to bear out the prophecy. What the mind is led to believe is what the eye will observe.

We tend to undervalue and fail to appreciate the absolutely incredible power of the human mind. When the human mind believes in something—anything—the belief acts as a stimulus to create the reality of whatever the mind believes. When is the last time you became victim to your own mind-set? You had it in your mind that you placed 20 dollars in the kitchen drawer that holds little things like glue and string and small appliance and flashlight batteries. Every year at the holiday season you give the man or woman, boy or girl, who delivers your newspaper a tip. You had it in mind to do it. Somehow you became distracted. Was it the phone, the doorbell, or perhaps even the dog barking to be let out? Doesn't matter. Your line of thought was interrupted. You did whatever was demanded of you, and you completely forgot about the 20 dollars. Of course, at some later time when you sat down to write a note and include the money in an envelope you went to the kitchen drawer, and the 20 dollars was nowhere to be found. "Did someone steal it? Where did I put it? I know I put it right here in this drawer." In your mind you put the money in the drawer. That was your intention. You honestly believe that you did. You have a mind-set. Reality is created by your belief.

A friend confessed to me once that on a bird-watching outing he was predisposed to see a Baltimore oriole. Orioles were rare in this locale, and he especially wanted to see what his neighbor had told him, i.e., that there were several Orioles in the vicinity. Before long he spotted the oriole. He fixed his binoculars on the bird and said "Yes!" "No, it isn't," said his wife. "That is not an oriole." "Yes it is," replied my friend. Only after another careful look through the binoculars did my friend admit that he had wanted to see the oriole so badly that he'd probably jumped to the wrong conclusion. In truth, the eye sees what the mind believes.

Beliefs can command our behavior and our very lives. On September 11, 2001, a group of believers carried out a terrorist mission such as has never been seen before on planet Earth. The content of their belief is now well known. Suffice it to say that according to their belief system, they were assuring for themselves the blessing of future life and reward with Allah. They methodically prepared and trained for their mission, and except for United Airlines Flight 93, which was forced down over Shanksville, Pennsylvania, they carried it out flawlessly.

Sam Harris makes a strong comment on the power of belief in some sort of afterlife. "What one believes happens after death dictates much of what one believes about life, and this is why faith-based religion, in presuming to fill in the blanks in our knowledge of the hereafter, does such heavy lifting for those who fall under its power. A single proposition—you will not die—once believed, determines a response to life that would be otherwise unthinkable."[9]

Belief can also be the key variable in our quest for healing, both physical and emotional. A woman, suffering from a flow of blood for over 12 years, cuts through the crowd in order to touch Jesus' garment. She touches him. "Daughter, your faith has made you well; go in peace, and be healed of your disease." [10]Regardless of the authenticity of the passage, the point is made: the mind's intensity of belief brings about the desired result.

---

[9] Sam Harris, *The End of Faith: Religion, Terror, and the Future of Reason* (New York: W. W. Norton, 2004) 38.

[10] Mark 5: 24b-34; According to the *Jesus Seminar*, this is likely an added scenario, not authentic Jesus material.

Many people are familiar with the biblical story of Samson and Delilah.[11] Samson believed the secret of his strength was in his long hair. He held this belief intently, with all his heart and mind. He finally gives into the seductive entreaty of Delilah and foolishly tells her of his secret: "A razor has never come upon my head." When he falls asleep, Delilah sees to it that Samson's hair is cut. Upon awakening, Samson finds himself weak like any other man, no longer the strong man. Of course he was weak! He had betrayed his own belief.

Perhaps in the same vein, but with a different twist, is the account of a former student, a 20-year-old young woman, who, by consensus of the men and women in the seminar of about 14 people, was believed to be beautiful by almost any common standard of physical beauty. Nevertheless, she rigidly held to an image of herself as pudgy and definitively unattractive. Reality, to her, was a negative physical self-image, while to the class members and myself, the reality was of pronounced physical beauty and attractiveness. She believed she was borderline ugly, and that is what she saw when she looked in a mirror. Believing is seeing.

In a sense, the entire world of medicine and the effectiveness of pharmaceutical prescriptions depend on belief. The placebo has a grand history, without which modern medicine would be in a state of disarray. The placebo depends on the belief by the patient that the pill is the real thing and will be efficacious. Often, to the extent of the belief that a prescribed pill actually has the potential to bring about healing, the patient will show marked improvement. The conclusion is clear and unequivocal: medical improvement is due to the belief of the mind, not to the sugar-based placebo.

Radical Constructivism as Mental Process

I shall adopt Ernst von Glasersfeld's definition of radical constructivism. Glasersfeld is one of the foremost modern thinkers in the development of constructivist thought,

> *(Constructivism)* is an unconventional approach to the problem of knowledge and knowing. It starts from the assumption that knowledge, no matter how it is defined, is in the heads of persons, and that the thinking subject has no alternative but to construct what he or she knows on the basis of his or her own experience. What we make of experience constitutes the only world we consciously live

---

[11] Judges 16:15–20;

in. It can be sorted into many kinds, such as things, self, others, and so on. But all kinds of experience are essentially subjective, and though I may find reasons to believe that my experience may not be unlike yours, I have no way of knowing that it is the same. The experience and interpretation of language are no exception.[12]

Objective reality cannot be known other than through the operational processes of the mind. This simple statement has served as the main point of philosophical inquiry for several thousand years.

The realist will say: "You are all wet about that. Of course objective reality can be known. Here is a piece of lumber. I shall rap my knuckle on it. I may even hit you over the head with it. How can you say that it cannot be known?"

I am not saying that this piece of lumber does not exist or that it is a figment of your imagination. I am not saying that it won't hurt me if you hit me over the head with it. I am saying that apart from the processes of your mind, there is no way you can know that this piece of lumber is real. It is your mind and its functioning processes that lead you to interpret, create, invent, or perceive this piece of lumber. Of course you call the lumber real! You see that it is a beautiful piece of white pine. It is 5/8 inch thick, six inches wide, and 36 inches long. It is well planed and has no knots. Your experience of this board is related to other experiences of this kind of wood because you are an experienced carpenter. You intend to cut this board into two equal pieces in length for use as shelves in your newly designed kitchen pantry.

I am saying that you would have no knowledge of this piece of so-called *real* wood if it were not for the experience of your senses, which are processed in turn by your nervous system and its tie-in to the functions of your brain. I may have a completely different experience of this piece of white pine. First of all, the word *board* is simply a convention of language, as is also the identifying term *white pine*. The measurements are all a matter of commonly agreed upon convention. They are not inherently a part of the piece of wood. Also, my experience with wood of this sort is negative, in that it was just this sort of lumber that dropped off the truck in front of me on the highway. I swerved to avoid running over it, but I caught the end of it and it punctured my tire. I was fortunate not to lose control of my car.

---

[12] Ernst von Glasersfeld, *Radical Constructivism: A Way of Knowing and Learning* (London: Falmer Press, 1995).

So I must say to the "realist" that while I do not dispute that the board exists, my experience with this piece of wood may be drastically different from your experience of the same piece of wood. More important, my ensuing reality will be somewhat different from your ensuing reality. The reality of the board is the immediate result of each of our constructed realities. My mental construct is different from your mental construct.

The same reasoning process is related to the wooden chair in my study at the university. Some students liked the chair. Others thought it was unattractive and uncomfortable. Likewise, the same reasoning may apply to your pick-up truck, as well as to my old knockabout. And certainly such reasoning and logic apply to matters of faith and belief and how we interpret and understand ultimate reality, ultimate being, and the concept of God.

Sam Harris, in his book *The End of Faith*, describes the mental process: "The world that you see and hear is nothing more than a modification of your consciousness, the physical status of which remains a mystery. Your nervous system sections the undifferentiated buzz of the universe into separate channels of sight, sound, smell, taste, and touch, as well as other senses of lesser renown—proprioceptors (*specialized nerve endings in muscles, tendons, and joints*), kinesthesia, enteroreception (*entero refers to intestines*), and even echolocation. The sights and sounds and pulsings that you experience at this moment are like different spectra of light thrown forth by the prism of the brain."[13] (Italics added.)

After reading to this point, most of us will likely respond that we do not remember constructing anything. We think we are fairly objective in our thoughts and assessments, in our opinions and beliefs. We think we have a solid view of reality and the world about us, even the world of religion and faith. At this point, let us turn to the thought of Jean Piaget and his theory of how children come to experience and interpret the world around them.

---

[13] Harris, *End of Faith*, 41.

Chapter Two

Constructivism II: How We Learn

Jean Piaget was both a developmental psychologist and a cognitive psychologist. He observed children in their natural or everyday habitats rather than in a laboratory designed for the study of behavior. His basic research questions were how do children learn? and how do they know? (that is, how do they generate knowledge?). Piaget came to postulate four basic stages of human mental and behavioral development. Each stage builds upon what was learned in the previous stage. No stage is skipped over.

In the first stage, from birth to about two, the sensorimotor stage, the child learns through sensory impressions and motor activity. In this stage, characterized by simple play, the tiny child begins to learn to control his/her body movements, as well as objects in the external world. At about five to seven months, a baby will cry if you show him/her an object of interest and then hide it from sight. During this stage, the child slowly comes to realize that even though objects are out of sight, they still exist. Thus, the child enjoys games where the object is temporarily hidden from its gaze. This translates into object permanence. When object permanence is achieved, the parent becomes an ongoing part of the child's life even though the parent is out of the room or otherwise out of sight.

In the pre-operational stage between ages two and six, the child begins to manipulate images and symbols. Almost any object can be imagined to be an airplane or a missile as the child swishes it though the air while holding it in his/her hand. A broom handle can become a horse. A cardboard box can become a kitchen, a stove, or a dwelling. A toy train takes on human characteristics as it puffs up a sofa or stuffed chair. Language quickly enters the picture. Children often name inanimate objects, be they teddy bears or blankets. Imaginative thought begins at this time, characterized by pretend games.

THE FLIPSIDE OF GODSPEAK

The concrete operational stage, from six or seven to about 11 years, shows markedly less egocentrism, as the child begins to understand a situation from the viewpoint or perspective of another child. During this stage, the child learns the beginning of logical thought, but more in terms of concrete objects than of ideas or propositions. The early discipline of arithmetic is basic to all later mathematical calculations. Grasp of such concepts as weight, length, height, and mass are typical of the early years of this period. Slowly the elemental processes evolve into more advanced categories of thought wherein the child is able to combine various concepts, such as space and time, or hold simultaneous ideas pertaining to width and length.

The fourth stage, formal operations, coincides with the beginning of adolescence and continues throughout life. This stage marks the beginning of logical thought and the ability to deal with abstract ideas and concepts such as truth, justice, goodness, and beauty. The adolescent quickly finds herself/himself experiencing the body changes that are a part of puberty and for the first time is challenged with concepts such as moral/ethical values in the conduct and pursuit of relationships with the other sex. In short, in this stage the adolescent enters the adult world of abstract reasoning in all of its dimensions. Skills in probability theory, analogue thinking, problem solving, scientific experimentation, musical prowess and composition, and second-language development are developed, honed, and polished, sometimes into a lasting vocation.

During these developmental sequences, three basic principles are at work, which Piaget calls assimilation, accommodation, and equilibration. The basic process is the child's increasing ability to organize his/her daily experiences. Assimilation is the taking-in process. It has to do with the absorbing of information from the senses and the daily world of experience, beginning at the earliest sensorimotor and preoperational stages. Assimilation will continue throughout the lifespan.

Most of the time assimilation is not a problem. The new information just seems to be absorbed and fits right in with the child's growing view and experience of the world. But frequently the assimilation of new experience or information causes a conflict with ideas or concepts that have already been assimilated, and the child is forced to do something about resolving the conflict. To do something about it is what Piaget calls accommodation. The new information must be somehow brought into harmony with what has already been assimilated. This sometimes requires unlearning and re-learning. The new knowledge is brought onto the scene, and the child seeks to accommodate this new knowledge to the old knowledge. An obvious example of this occurs when the child begins to question the story about Santa Claus. The child has assimilated this story, and as the child begins to interact with others, and also begins to question, he/she will invariably learn to accommodate the new material to the old material. The end result of this accommodation of the old and new material will satisfy until a new conflict comes into play, at which point a new accommodation is called for. Eventually the assimilated Santa Claus material is written off as a fairy tale or a myth. As Piaget indicates, accommodation involves either the revision of an old schema (structure) or the creation of a new schema in one's knowledge reservoir. Piaget labels the continuing process of balancing assimilation with accommodation as the process of equilibration.

Constructivists and constructivism have increasingly claimed the pioneering work of Piaget as the foundation of an epistemological paradigm. The constructivist goal or purpose is not to create a true picture of reality or of the world or the universe (so-called objective reality), but rather to describe the way the human organism organizes its own experience. Constructivism claims that everything outside ourselves that we call reality is our experience of life. It is our *invented* or *created* reality. In this sense, we *generate* rather than *discover* knowledge.

According to Ernst von Glasersfeld, until Piaget, the experimental and the behaviorist paradigms of the early twentieth century were the "in thing" in psychology.

> Psychology was now defined as "the science of behavior," and for radical behaviorists, the mind, the entire world of concepts, meanings, purposes, intentions, and indeed knowledge was discarded as a bunch of pre-scientific, mentalistic superstitions. . . . Piaget's approach also went counter to well established ideas in philosophy. Most philosophers considered knowledge as a static entity. Knowledge, for them, was *there*, ready to be *discovered*. The notion that individuals could *generate* knowledge, and that one could specify the processes involved in its production, was not a notion that fitted the traditional pattern.[1]

In Piaget's thought, the human mind is the supreme creator of reality because the mind designs and creates the structures that help us organize and hence make sense of data generated by the senses and by everyday human experience. Von Glasersfeld comments on how this concept flies in the face of the so-called realists:

---

[1] Ernst von Glasersfeld, "Homage to Jean Piaget (1896–1980)," *Irish Journal of Psychology* 18 (3) (1997) 293–306.

for whom the essence of science lies in the collecting of "objective" data which, they believe, speak for themselves and automatically provide true explanations. Knowledge, for them, is the result of discovery. On the other side is Piaget's constructivism, for which all science is the product of a thinking mind's conceptualization. From this perspective, knowledge does not "represent" or depict an independent reality but is a collection of inventions that happen to fit the world as it is experienced.[2]

This experiencing of the world is, of course, what initially begins to appear in the sensorimotor stage, between birth and two years of age, as described earlier. "For Piaget they (our concepts of space and time) are constructs whose build-up begins very early, namely in the course of what he called 'circular reactions' during the first two years of the infant's cognitive development. The concepts of space and time arise in conjunction with those of object permanence and causality."[3] Von Glasersfeld goes on to comment that "in Piaget's theory of cognition . . . the mind primarily assimilates, that is, it perceives and categorizes experience in terms that are already known. Only if the result of this process causes a hitch and creates a perturbation, a review is initiated that may lead to an *accommodation*. That is to say, it may give rise to change in an existing structure or the formation of a new one."[4]

Von Glasersfeld claims that traditional psychologists have always had difficulty assimilating Piaget's theories into traditional ideas, and the most difficult part of Piaget's thought that continues *not* to fit into traditional psychology is "the constructivist principle that we ourselves build our picture of the world in which we live."[5] In order to illustrate how we do this, I shall ask the reader to perform with me a brief exercise.

Tell Me About Your Family

Here is the situation. Since we all come from a family of origin, this should be an exercise that is easy to identify with. Pretend that you are interviewing the Hopkins family—mother, father, daughter and son. The family is sitting in the room with you, and you ask each family member to tell you

---

[2] Ibid.
[3] Ibid.
[4] Ibid.
[5] Ibid.

how it was living in this family day by day. A good way to start the conversation may be to say "Please introduce me to your family."

Then invite each member to describe in as much detail as possible the daily problems, challenges, and rewards that were common to this family. All remarks are to be addressed to you, the interviewer, with the others remaining silent while you interact with each family member.

Imagine that you have completed this exercise and have allowed each participant adequate time to describe and explain all of his or her experiences.

Here are my questions and comments to you, the interviewer: How many families did you just interview? Were you surprised at the different "realities" that were described?

Traditional wisdom says that you interviewed four members of one family. However, nobody described the one and only objectively real family. There is no objectively real family. If there were, who's objectively real family would it be? Father's? Mother's? Daughter's? Son's?

Is the one true objectively real family the one you create as you listen to the four family members tell their story? After all, the interviewer sits in the catbird seat and is ostensibly more objective than any of the family members and thus able to meld the various descriptions into a single piece of whole fabric. Or has the interviewer (you, the observer) become part of what has been observed, i.e., have you become swept up into each of the four descriptions of the family to such an extent that you now experience empathic feelings connected with each of the four participants?

I submit that you are *not* dealing with one true objective family. You are dealing with *four* families, each with four persons related to each other by birth or law, yet each person having described to you the family that they either formed by marriage or were born or adopted into and now experience on a daily basis. None of these four familial descriptions is identical to the other three. This is because each person has described to you, the interviewer, the family that they internalized and from which they constantly assimilated new material and then made appropriate mental accommodations to, which in turn enabled each individual to make sense out of his/her own life experiences.

The point is that while there may be an objective "family" that is known to the government and the Internal Revenue Service as the Hopkins family, there are, in fact, four different families. This is because each of the four persons has organized in their mind certain schemas and structures that were then exposed to ongoing assimilations and necessary accommodations. The result is that each family member has constructed his/her own family. In other words, each family member has created or built or invented a reality that is different from the realities of the other three members. While the four realities may involve the same four people, there is no possible way each person could experience the same reality. Such differences as gender, age, birth order, education, prior experience of the parents in their respective families of origin, and the social realities of employment and community status all combine to form different social and familial realities for each of the four family members. These are not merely differing perceptions of one objective reality, the Hopkins family. Rather, they are four different realities, or four different creations of reality.[6]

As long as we understand that the observer is always a participant in what is observed and cannot be separated from it, we will be in a position to be active participants in the creation and invention of knowledge, not mere discoverers.

There is no objective reality. There is only invented, created, or constructed reality, our experience of whatever it is we would like to think is objectively real. As an example, please consider the experience of driving a car and the so-called "rules of the road." Each of us, according to our own acquisition and creation of knowledge, has organized our "automobile driving world" around certain rules and principles, one of which is that when the light turns red, it is safer and healthier for each respective driver to stop. In this case our individual perceptive realities all agree with respect to the assigned meaning of red and green lights. Our collective agreement becomes more than a social convention. It becomes law.

Likewise, to a large extent the stability of our world and the stability of our civilization depend upon the general agreement of our experienced realities. This agreement of realities is really an agreement of our quest for knowledge in physics, mathematics, biology, and chemistry, to name but a few of the basic disciplines.

In summary, constructivism involves the assimilation of knowledge based on experience and sensory input. When previously assimilated material comes into conflict with incoming data, an accommodation is negotiated within the mind, thus helping the individual to resolve the conflict. Each new resolution of conflict, i.e., each new accommodation, becomes part of an ongoing, lifelong process of equilibration. As a result of this equilibration, we are involved in a lifelong construction process wherein we essentially build our own perceptions, images, and mental creations. Each of us

---

[6] Richard Chasin et al. *One Couple: Four Realities* (New York: The Guilford Press, 1990).

must do this for himself/herself. Nobody can do it for us. Constructivism is the ongoing creation that becomes the driving force of life and growth.

Summing Up

Constructivism

1. Is concerned with what we believe and how we come to believe it.
2. Does not deny reality or that there is such a thing as reality.
3. Claims that it is impossible to know reality directly.
4. Claims that reality can only be known via the agency of a processing organism, i.e., the mind.
5. Claims that mind does not discover reality.
6. Claims that the mind invents, creates, and builds thought processes that attempt to comprehend reality.
7. Claims that objective reality is inseparable from the observing/participating-experiencing mind.
8. Claims the observing mind always becomes part of what is observed.
9. Owes a great debt to psychologist Jean Piaget, who postulated and described the mental processes of assimilation and accommodation.
10. Is functionally dependent on assimilation, i.e. the gathering into the mind the sum total of human experiences and the information transmitted by the senses.
11. Further depends on accommodation, the process by which the mind attempts to resolve conflict due to ongoing assimilation of new experience that clashes with earlier assimilated material.
12. Utilizes Piaget's accommodation as the process of creating new schemas that will eliminate conflict between earlier and more recent assimilation.
13. Is the mental process that revises old schemas and builds new schemas, resulting in ever increasing equilibrations.
14. Is thus the process by which the cognitive organism constantly constructs new realities.
15. Is thus the creating, inventing, and organizing of new experiences resulting in new constructs, a cumulative process that continues throughout life.
16. Is thus the belief that we ourselves build, invent, and create what we call "reality."

Chapter Three

The Quest for Truth

WHAT IS truth? Is truth different from reality? Are there kinds and levels of truth? Is there a difference between scientific truth and religious or philosophical truth? What do we mean when we say, "Tell the truth?" What do we mean when we talk about truth in advertising? Do statistics tell the truth, or can they be misleading and deceiving? What is the difference between truth and little white lies? The traditional court oath, "Do you swear to tell the truth, the whole truth, and nothing but the truth?" is, of course, ridiculous, because it's impossible for anyone to know "the whole truth" and to be positive his/her statements contain "nothing but the truth."

Perhaps the most important questions to ask are: Is there a relationship between truth and reality, and, if so, what is that relation? To what extent is truth *dependent* upon a subject or an observer? To what extent is truth *independent* of a subject or an observer? Your truth may not be my truth. Your reality may not be my reality. What is the individual's role in determining truth? What is the absolute and objective truth, the truth that has to do with the way things really are?

We begin our quest for truth by reminding ourselves that constructivism does not deny that there is such a thing as objective reality. Constructivism says only that human beings cannot possess any direct or final knowledge of this reality. Call it what you will, universal truth, God truth, creation of the universe truth, ultimate reality truth, or metaphysical truth, the fact remains that we cannot go beyond the limits of our humanness. We simply do not have the knowledge to comprehend ultimate truth, any more than we can comprehend ultimate reality. Achieving this kind of truth has been the goal and purpose of philosophy, theology, physics, and math for centuries. Yet we remain trapped within the creative and inventive ability of our minds. Constructivists hold that we do not *discover* truth, because this implies that truth is "out there" waiting for us to discover it or stumble upon it. Rather, constructivism is the invention and creation of reality. "We create the world we live in and then live in the world we created."[1] We can only appropriate what we believe to be true by hypothesizing, theorizing, and creating laboratory models and designs, but we cannot *know* in any final and absolute sense. There may be significant evidence in support of certain theories, such as evolution and relativity (as compared to other theories and hypotheses), yet this does not qualify as absolute proof or absolute knowledge.[2]

In addition to individual frames of reference, preconceived bias, and conceptual frameworks, there are several schools of thought regarding how we should approach the study of truth. *Correspondence* theory, *coherence* theory, and *consensus* are the three I shall discuss most fully here.

Correspondence Theory of Truth

The correspondence theory of truth is the most favored of the several theories.[3] It basically says that if what you believe to be true about anything (current events, math, physics, art, music, etc.) corresponds to the objective facts of reality, then truth is established. Thus, if I believe that the butler killed Miss Plum in the study with a wrench, and if this can be born out by the facts, then my belief is true. The test of truth is its agreement or *correspondence* with reality.

Randall and Buchler state: "A Belief is true if the ideas contained in it correspond to objects as they are in fact. This view has not merely been held by many philosophers but seems to conform rather closely to our ordinary

---

[1] Carl Ehlert "The Search For Truth," from a sermon delivered at the Unitarian-Universalist Church, Danville, Ind., Feb. 19, 2006.

[2] The so-called "intelligent design" advocates and the scientific creationists use the term "theory" in a very loose and irresponsible manner. They claim that evolutionary "theory" is not proven and that evolutionists should put their theory up for debate and comparison with creationism and intelligent design theories. This position fails to understand the scientific method of research, in that in order for a theory to be viable, it must have withstood many challenging hypotheses. Only when hypotheses are established in a statistical analysis are they utilized in theory-building. Creationism and intelligent design propositions are not theories in any scientific sense of the word: They are nothing more than untested and untestable hypotheses. One of the first rules of scientific inquiry is that hypotheses must be testable. Once a hypothesis is established (in the sense that it has failed of rejection) it is constantly challenged by ongoing replication in ongoing experiments.

[3] David Marian, "The Correspondence Theory of Truth," *The Stanford Encyclopedia of Philosophy* (Summer 2002).

common sense usage when we speak of truth. The flaws in the definition arise when we ask what is meant by 'agreement' or 'correspondence' of ideas and objects, belief and facts, thoughts and reality. In order to test the truth of an idea or belief we must presumably compare it with the reality in some sense."[4] As another writer expressed it, "Truth is a very simple and handy concept. It is the correspondence of a pictorial or symbolic representation to the thing being represented."[5]

Of course, one can make this theory sound attractive by using the simplest of illustrations. However, when we get into deeper issues and questions, the correspondence theory may not appear to be so easy.

- What is the truth about the effect of cholesterol on stroke and heart disease?
- What is the truth about black holes in the universe?
- What is the truth about Stonehenge?
- What is the truth about the effect of liberalism on the mores of people?
- What is the truth about the effect of conservatism on the mores of people?
- What is the truth about the origins of the universe?
- What is the truth of Buddhism?
- What is the truth of Islam?
- What is the truth of Christianity?

This same line of thought may be applied to such issues as abortion, euthanasia, stem cell research, social welfare, environmental pollution, global warming, acid rain, and mining and drilling for natural resources.

In order to answer any of these questions, it is necessary to get as close to the most recent and authoritative knowledge as possible. But which authorities are accepted and fully respected as being universal, valid, and absolute? The creationist school of thought posits authoritative answers based on the Hebrew Torah. Islam has the Koran, and Christianity has the Bible. Then there are the Vedas of Hinduism and the Tao Te Ching of Taoism. To what extent are all of these based on assumptions of authority?

Appeals to authority are not enough to establish truth. The question remains: Whose authority? Which authority? On what basis can one authority be positioned above or below any other authority?

---

[4] John Herman Randall Jr. and Justus Buchler, *Philosophy: An Introduction* (New York: Barnes and Noble, 1942) 133.
[5] Peter B. Lloyd, *What Is Truth?* http://easyweb.easynet.co.uk/~ursa/philos/cert04.htm.

Scholarship and intellectual pursuits usually end up as publications in scholarly journals. Journals pervade the world of the academician, be they journals of engineering, physics, medicine, human development, psychology, sociology, anthropology, literature, or the arts. In addition, there are numerous subdivisions within each discipline. Then there is the question of which journals in the same discipline or subdiscipline are the most highly respected. Which journals are more prestigious, and which are reputed to contain reports of higher quality research endeavors?

As the reader can appreciate, the correspondence theory of truth is more complicated than it first appears. From a constructivist point of view, the problem with the correspondence theory is that correspondence with fact/reality is impossible, inasmuch as fact/reality can be known only via the human mind and its mental processes (Piaget's assimilation, accommodation, and resulting equilibration.) Therefore, in the final analysis, while there may be such a thing as objective truth, it cannot be known or appropriated except by the thought processes of the mind. This is the theme of the constructivists, who maintain that reality and truth are of the same order and neither exists independently, objectively, and universally. Truth, much like reality, is a product of the interconnecting and filtering processes of the human brain.

Coherence Theory of Truth

The word coherence refers to a sticking-together quality; it implies congruence and consistency. Coherence theorists hold that truth can be defined only when one proposition is demonstrated to *cohere* with other propositions or sets of propositions. Consistency is key to the concept of coherence theory. The coherence theory of truth builds its case not on the degree of coherence with reality, but on coherence or consistency with a set or sets of propositions that address and relate to the same phenomenon. According to Randall and Buchler, whenever a new belief coheres better with the great bulk of our experience and knowledge than an older belief or body of knowledge, then the older belief must be abandoned, either in part or in whole.[6]

Coherence theory is a product of philosophical idealism, and it is based on the epistemological belief that we cannot know reality except through the intervening perception of our mental facility. "Another epistemological argument for coherence theory is based on the view that we cannot 'get

---

[6] Randall and Buchler, *Philosophy: An Introduction* 135.

outside' our set of beliefs and compare propositions to objective facts . . . This argument . . . depends on a coherence theory of justification. The argument infers from such a theory that we can only know that a proposition coheres with a set of beliefs. We can never know that a proposition corresponds to reality."[7]

At one point in time, people believed the earth was flat. This was the prevailing belief of humankind. Advocates of correspondence theory claimed that flatness was reality. Of course this could not be demonstrated. It was more an article of faith. Advocates of coherence theory no doubt claimed that flatness was consistent with a set of prevailing propositions about the nature of the universe. Copernicus and later Galileo claimed that the sun was the center of the solar system. Did Copernicus have a correspondence theory of truth, claiming that the heliocentric belief was in correspondence with reality? Or was Copernicus an advocate of coherence? Since no one else (except Galileo) could have provided Copernicus with a proposition with which Copernicus could disagree or agree, Copernicus likely claimed that the heliocentric universe corresponded with reality. The same would hold for Galileo. The fact that Galileo eventually recanted was due in large measure to the situation that no one could be found who shared his hypothesis, i.e., that the earth revolved around the sun. In modern times, the heliocentric view of the universe is no longer a hypothesis. It is theory established by constant replication of observable data. As such, we accept as true the belief that the earth revolves around the sun. This belief is based on both correspondence theory and coherence theory because there is ample evidence from astronomical sources as well as space exploration (correspondence) and consistency of propositional truth, hypotheses and theories amounting to a body of science (coherence).

The key difference between coherence and correspondence is that coherence deals with the consistency of propositions and hypotheses in their agreement with each other, whereas correspondence deals with a consistency of events or propositions in their agreement with what is conceived as being reality. Correspondence as a test of truth points to consistency when comparing alleged events with so-called facts. Coherence is a studied and tested agreement among significant statements purporting to support the same conclusion. Coherence theory relates to a set or sets of hypotheses. These are then tested and scrutinized for accuracy and then form a set or sets of theories.

---

[7] James O. Young. "The Coherence Theory of Truth," *The Stanford Encyclopedia of Philosophy* (Summer 2001).

THE FLIPSIDE OF GODSPEAK

Truth by Consensus

If 99 people out of 100 believe that humankind (Neil Armstrong et al.) has landed on the moon, then it must be true. This is simple consensus.

Coherence, with its emphasis on consistency with propositions, should not be confused with consensus. Consensus is manifestly not valid for a large number of beliefs about such things as ghosts, benign or malevolent spirits, extraterrestrial beings, or even gods/deities. Consistency is one thing. Consensus is another. If we lived by consensus, we would perhaps have to declare that God exists, the Koran is true, the Bible is true, goblins exist, extraterrestrials exist, the devil exists, human life begins at conception, and all nondemocratic governments on earth are evil. This is because consensus may be reduced to the simple belief that truth is nothing more or less than prevailing public opinion. Even if 99.9 percent of people within the United States believe in a theistic-type God, that alone does not make it true.

Nevertheless, truth by consensus is a necessary thing for civilized people. It enables the rule of law and social interaction. It helps bring about social conventions that perhaps make life more enjoyable and less dangerous. It can also be a dangerous thing, especially if it is used to generalize from the beliefs of a few to a prescribed way of life for the many. In countless instances, we use consensus as an easy test of truth. Even though it can be extremely dangerous, we hold to the hypothesis that vast numbers of people simply cannot be wrong.

Let us conclude the discussion of these three theories of truth by acknowledging that most of us use all three types of truth in our everyday lives. We use correspondence in medical diagnoses, courts of law, and countless other practical matters. Perhaps without being aware of it, we insist that the facts as we understand them correspond to what is alleged to be the reality of a situation?

And although we may use it less, the coherence test of truth holds sway when we depend on congruence between sets or several sets of propositions. Scholarly pursuits in fields such as physics, geology, anthropology, psychology, psychiatry, sociology, and economics result in research that produces a preponderance of significant evidence in favor of various hypotheses that, after testing, become part of theory. The work of some scholars and scientists seeks to bring the results of coherence tests into the domain of correspondence tests. Some medical and biological researchers endeavor to discover cures for different kinds of cancer by first utilizing coherence theory as a sine qua non for the establishment of greater degrees of certainty on the level of correspondence theory.

Finally, we use consensus in many day-by-day situations. Advertisers certainly abuse it when they make claims as to how many people are using a certain product. Republicans and Democrats use it when they claim consensus on issues, especially controversial ones.

Intuition, Pragmatism, Dogma, Revelation

There is also *intuitive* truth, *revealed* truth, *dogmatic* truth, and *pragmatic* truth. Dogma, however, is most usually related to revealed theology and is best considered as a part of revealed truth.

Intuitive truth is frequently the highest court of appeal in the quest for truth. As most of us have learned, it is difficult to contradict whatever beliefs a person holds based on intuition. *The Oxford Dictionary of Psychology* defines intuition as "immediate understanding, knowledge, or awareness, derived neither from perception nor from reasoning."[8] Randall and Buchler state, "Intuition as an independent and allegedly superior form of knowing represents the hunt for a royal road to knowledge."[9] Intuition as a royal road to knowledge is therefore a royal road to truth. But is intuition credible? Does it flow from empirical evidence of any description? Does it flow from logic or rational discourse? Inasmuch as intuition is a type of belief that is devoid of evidence and verified data we can hardly give it any status as a method of establishing truth. On an intuitive level, I may point to the vastness and wonder of nature and of the universe and then claim that God exists. I say to myself "I just know this is true. There must be a designer/creator." But this is neither a rational nor a necessarily logical belief. There are other explanations relating to the existence of the natural order that are far less intuitive and also cohere with scientific research. The debate about whether "intelligent design" is an acceptable theory for the formation of the universe hinges largely on two points: First, the argument from design to a designer; and second, intuition. The cornerstone of intuition and intuitive thinking is faith—faith that the intuitive thought I harbor in my mind would not be there were it not true. This is not only an irrefutable statement, it is extremely poor theology.

Revealed truth, the cornerstone of all authoritarian religions, claims that the ultimate author or ultimate authority reveals truth to humankind and it is the burden of humans to respond to it. Through known history

---

[8] Andrew M. Colman, *The Oxford Dictionary of Psychology* (Oxford: Oxford University Press, 2001).
[9] Ibid. 116.

THE FLIPSIDE OF GODSPEAK

there have been thousands of religions and religious spokespeople who claim that they speak for the deity or deities. Did God really dictate the words on the tablets of stone Moses transmitted to the masses? Are St. Paul, St. Augustine, Martin Luther, John Calvin, and the Pope correct as to their interpretation of the laws, morals, rituals, sacraments, and confessional statements that they claim as God's truth? Did Joseph Smith really receive the Book of Mormon from God somewhere near Elmira, New York? Did Mohammed really receive the Koran from God?

Too often, and to the detriment of humankind, spokespersons for supernatural authorities thrive on the dynamic of relying on ignorance in creating fear. When people fear and are afraid for their lives, they will readily believe the message of the authority and will be easily controlled by a theocratic prophet or ruler, perhaps even by a demagogue. The appeal to divine authority, with the promises of eternal or everlasting life beyond this world, with threats of hell and eternal damnation, is the stuff of which revealed religion is made.

In brief, revelation as a source of truth is not a philosophically viable option. If one puts faith and trust in the authority, there is no humanly possible way to verify the alleged truth. There simply is no empirically valid evidence. Grant the method and you cannot lose.

Pragmatic truth is determined and defined by its usefulness and/or its utility. If something works it is useful and if it is useful it is true. William James, John Dewey, C. S. Peirce, F. C. S. Schiller, and John Stuart Mill are the most well known advocates of pragmatism.

Folks who accept divine revelation and religious devotees who live their lives in line with prescribed pious practices and beliefs are more pragmatic in their assessment of truth than we tend to realize. When believers state that their faith brings them peace of mind, emotional security, comfort, joy, and a sense of purpose in life, they are being pragmatic. For the pragmatist, truth is what works and is useful. The rewards of faith prove the truth of the belief. Additionally, when believers hold to the truth of their revealed theology and also join together in expressing their faith in the company of dozens, hundreds, or even thousands of fellow believers, there is a triple "ticket" to truth. There is utilitarian pragmatism, there is revelation, and there is consensus. This "triple threat" approach to the truth is the chief reason religious conservatives and fundamentalists are difficult to reason with. They believe they know the truth, that they possess the truth, and that they are living the truth. In true pragmatic fashion, it works for them. As Sam Harris comments: "Religious faith represents so uncompromising a misuse of the power of our minds that it forms a kind of perverse, cultural singularity—a vanishing point beyond which rational discourse proves impossible." [10]

There are times when a person's intuition may prove to be lifesaving. However, there are other times when it may prove a nightmare. In sum, it is neither a reliable nor valid method of ascertaining truth.

First-Order Truth

In order to better understand the dilemma and challenge of separating truth from error in theological and philosophical endeavors, I propose to separate personal or subjective truth from so-called universal or objective truth. I shall henceforth arbitrarily distinguish between these two levels of truth as *first-order truth* and *second-order truth*.

First-order truth is relative, conditional, subjective, and personal. It is the "truth" each of us arrives at concerning the myriad of everyday events and thoughts that preoccupy our minds. This truth is not just the truth of how we see the world, it is the product of our minds as our minds construct, create, invent, and perceive the world around us. Perhaps you see it as a creation of some deity. If so, that is *your* truth. Perhaps I see it as the result of a big bang and a slow evolutionary process over millions of years. That is *my* truth. Truth in this sense is best defined as a person's attempt to create and invent a rendering or interpretation of reality as the person comes to understand that reality.

I cannot say that what you believe to be true is either true or not true. All I can say is that I either share or do not share your belief. I may see truth (my personal, first-order truth) as being something quite different from your personal, first-order truth. Further, you may disagree with my truth. You may cajole me, tease me, make fun of me, even ridicule me for what I believe, but you cannot negate my truth. The most you can do is state clearly and unequivocally that you do not share my beliefs, that you do not share my truth.

According to constructivism, we can never get beyond first-order truth because there is no way we can get out of our own created reality. We can come to some sound conclusions. We can discard the geocentric view of the solar system for the heliocentric view. Or we can discard Newton's view of the universe in favor of Einstein's view (i.e., discard Newton's theory in favor of Einstein's theory.) We do this based on the preponderance of

---

[10] Sam Harris, *The End of Faith: Religion, Terror, and the Future of Reason* (New York: W.W. Norton, 2004) 25.

significant evidence. We do not base this on so-called discovery of some ultimate and universal truth. This means that everything we presently hold as being true may in some future time (in view of new research) prove to be not true. Scientific research can never really prove the truth of a hypothesis. All it can do, and it is much indeed, is to reject competing hypotheses.

All first-order truth is relative and subjective. It can never be absolute and objective. Objective reality may be out there, but it remains beyond human knowledge. All reality is personal, in the sense that what is outside ourselves can be sensed and experienced only through the filtering process of our own human minds.

Second-Order Truth

Second-order truth is absolute and universal truth. It is truth above and beyond our personal first-order truth. As such, it is always and forever unattainable because it is impossible for human beings to get out of their own minds. Since all reality is transmitted and filtered via the human brain, there is no way any human being can get beyond the constructions, creations, and inventions of her/his own mind.

Philosophers may postulate the metaphysical existence of an uncaused first cause or of a prime designer of the universe. Jewish theologians may adhere to a belief that a messianic savior will one day arrive on the earthly scene. Christian theologians may adhere to a belief that a messianic supernatural force has "revealed itself" via the presence of its "son" becoming manifest as a human being. However, there is no possible way that any of these propositions can ever be verified. While there may be such a thing as "objective reality," there is no way this so-called reality can ever be known except as creations, constructs, and inventions of the human mind.

This leads to the conclusion that second-order reality is beyond the pale of human existence. While we can talk about it and speculate about it, we cannot *know* it in any final, meaningful, and ordinary sense of the word.

My beliefs give color and hue to my reality and what I see to be the truth. This plays into my belief about God and ultimate reality, whence the universe came and how it was brought into existence. But belief is not knowledge. The very essence of our varying beliefs about the nature of ultimate reality is that our beliefs are what we choose to embrace as working hypotheses. Our beliefs are not the same thing as knowledge.

I have a dear friend whom I shall call Dalton. Dalton holds that the Bible speaks the truth and that God simply IS. And Jesus is God's son and is part of the trinity with the Holy Spirit. Dalton believes that God is both transcendent and immanent. Dalton further likens God to a stern and loving father who is the creator of all life and worlds and yet is also involved directly in all human endeavors. Dalton believes his God is the source of all his strength and wisdom.

I do not question the fact that for Dalton these beliefs are his reality and his reality is his truth. But—and there is a *but*—I would point out that this truth for Dalton is personal, relative, conditional, and subjective. It is first-order truth. Dalton's beliefs say nothing about the actual structure of the universe, the galaxies, and all infinity of space and time. Nor do his beliefs say anything about whether or not there is such a thing as God or how this God came into existence in the first place. For whatever reason Dalton has come upon his beliefs about reality, these beliefs constitute his truth. I do not doubt that his truth works for him.

Dalton's truth works for him because he believes it with all his heart and mind. Psychologist Rollo May has emphasized that whether or not our beliefs and values hold for us and give meaning to our lives depends on whether or not and to what extent we truly believe in the truth of these beliefs and values.[11] The phenomenon of personal belief is extremely powerful. As mentioned earlier, on occasion we may believe because we see, but there are many instances wherein we see because we first believe.

My conclusion is that each of us lives by our own experiential reality, our own experiential truth. We must—and this is a must—understand that your reality and truth may not be my reality and truth. Actually, this belief stands at the heart of our democracy and ensures that we do not live in any kind of theocracy where the ruling oligarchy of theological prelates prescribes what we are to believe.

By way of summary, whatever my mind concludes as my first level personal truth is of no comfort or benefit to me unless in the depths of my being I also believe it to be the way ultimate reality actually is. Another way of saying this is that most people believe that their personal first-order truth is also universal second-order truth. This means that Dalton is very certain that his first-order belief system corresponds to the way ultimate reality really is. This is *faith*, not knowledge.

By the same token, I believe in my own first-order truth, and my everyday working hypothesis is that my first-order personal and subjective truth is very close to second order-truth. But like Dalton, I do not know this. It is simply my belief. I can only speculate about the nature of what

---

[11] Rollo May, *Man's Search For Himself* (New York: W.W. Norton, 1953) (Chapter Six, 152. Signet Paperback Edition, 1967).

THE FLIPSIDE OF GODSPEAK

I am calling ultimate reality because ultimate reality is unknowable in any final and objective sense of the word. As a constructivist, I do not believe that ultimate reality (or any other approximate synonym) is knowable. As close as I can come to objective reality is my belief in and acceptance of the subjective creations, inventions, and constructs of my own mind.

Chapter Four

Is There Really God?
Faith Versus Knowledge

IN THE previous three chapters, I have held with a strong sense of consistency that reality cannot be known directly. And so it comes as no surprise that ultimate reality cannot be known directly. Whatever is *up there* or *out there*, if anything, cannot be known directly, but only as a creation, invention, or construction of the human mind. Furthermore, I have held that while people may have a sense of their own personal truth about ultimate reality, or first-order truth, it is impossible for these same persons to have firm knowledge of second-order truth. These persons may have *beliefs* that make up their *faith* about ultimate reality. This is first-order truth. This is their personal truth. But they cannot possibly have *knowledge* of the second order. It is simply unattainable.

In short, this means that no one has any genuine knowledge about God, at least under the definition of second-order truth. A believer may have faith that such a deity exists, but this is not knowledge. By the same token, no one has any definitive second-order knowledge that such a deity does *not* exist. This is precisely why the position of the positive or strong atheist is ultimately beyond proof.[1] Theism and positive atheism are both beyond the pale of human existence, and as such both are unknowable in any ordinary definition of knowledge. Negative (or weak*)* atheism states: "I do not believe in God." This is a statement about the belief system of the person who is making the statement. It is not a denial of a theistic or deistic God. It is a statement of faith. Positive atheism states: "I believe there is no

---

[1] Atheism is popularly thought of as *not* believing in God. In a less popular, yet more accurate, sense, atheism is the belief that there is *no God*. This difference, though subtle, is important. Both definitions are acceptable. *Merriam-Webster's Collegiate Dictionary* defines it as: 2a: a disbelief in the existence of deity, and 2b: the doctrine that there is no deity.

God." This statement, while also a statement of belief, goes further than the former statement in that it constitutes a denial that God exists. Therefore the latter statement (I believe there is *no* God) is a stronger statement and it requires a leap of faith into the unknown. Positive atheism ventures into that realm of belief that must remain forever a matter of faith rather than knowledge. As such, it suffers from the same limitations as theism.[2]

Agnosticism

Many people think of agnosticism as a station between theism and atheism. This is unfortunate, because the etymology of these words makes their meaning quite clear: theism is from the Greek *theo*, God; and atheism is from Greek *a*, without, and *theo*, God; while agnosticism is from Greek *a*, without, and *gnosis*, knowledge. Agnosticism is a formal philosophical/theological position claiming that ultimate reality is neither known nor knowable. To be an agnostic is to claim that it is not possible to have knowledge about the reality of a God or Gods. *Christian agnosticism* and *agnostic Christian* are contradictions in terms, inasmuch as the basic Christian core message, the kerygma (the early Christian proclamation that Jesus is Lord), is based on the belief that God has revealed himself through a Son who is believed to be the Christ. One can hardly hold this view and at the same time claim to be agnostic about the meaning of the Christ event. Perhaps a Christian believer could claim to be a *skeptical* believer or a *skeptical* Christian, but skepticism is different from agnosticism.

An agnostic is akin to a constructivist insofar as both terms are ontological and epistemological in nature, having to do with the questions what do we know? and how do we know? As we have seen, the constructivist claims that all knowledge is the product of mental processes wherein we construct, invent, or create what we think to be reality and that it is impossible to get beyond these mental constructs. An ontological and epistemological agnostic concurs with the constructivist to the extent that the agnostic claims to be without knowledge of anything beyond sensory input and experience. Therefore, to the thoroughgoing agnostic, knowledge of the ultimate is impossible.

---

[2] *The Atheism Web*, "More on definitions of atheism," http://www.infidels.org/news/atheism/sn-definitions.html. This brief article serves as a very concise review of the two definitions of atheism. Also see: Gordon Stein, *An Anthology of Atheism and Rationalism* (Amherst, N.Y., Prometheus, 1980) 3.

Is Faith a Way of Knowing?

Faith is belief or trust. It is not knowledge. One of the most famous definitions of faith comes from the New Testament book of Hebrews: "Now faith is the assurance of things hoped for, the conviction of things not seen." (Hebrews 11:1 RSV) In its usual meaning, faith deals with things that are beyond the realm of knowledge. Things *hoped for* and things *not seen* are outside the sphere of research. Faith as a method of epistemological inquiry must always be suspect. Following are three definitions of faith, each defining faith as a form of belief.

1. Faith as belief *in spite of* evidence to the contrary. In this sense faith is holding a belief in the face of preponderant evidence that indicates the belief to be false. As philosophers Randall and Buchler state: "It is emotionally more comfortable to cling to the beliefs one already holds than to be troubled by doubts, or to be faced with the need of revising one's habits of thought in the light of new evidence that they are unsound. On this attitude therefore one adopts only beliefs compatible with those already held, regarding new evidence with hostility and suspicion; and when confronted by allegedly new evidence, refusing to interpret it as such. Belief in spite of evidence thus goes hand in hand with the avoidance of evidence. In fact, the avoidance is absolutely essential. For we cannot safeguard ourselves against doubts if we leave ourselves open to their influence."[3] One of the hallmarks of some conservatives and all fundamentalists is belief in spite of evidence to the contrary.

An example of this type of faith is the literal belief held by creationists in the seven-day account of creation as related in Genesis 1:1-2:4a from the P or Priestly tradition referred to in Appendix I.[4] Creationists also hold to the second creation account, Genesis 2:4b – 3:24, which contains a different rendition of creation. This J or Jehovah tradition includes the narrative of Adam and Eve in the Garden of Eden, replete with the disobedience

---

[3] John Herman Randall, Jr., and Justus Buchler, *Philosophy: An Introduction* (New York: Barnes and Noble, 1942) 47–48.

[4] Henry Snyder Gehman, *The New Westminster Dictionary of the Bible*. (Philadelphia: The Westminster Press, 1970) 727–733.(See "Pentateuch"). The Documentary Theory in Biblical criticism holds that the Pentateuch is composed of four basic strands or layers of writing stemming from four basic traditions. *J* stands for the *Jehovah (Yahweh)* source. *E* stands for the *Elohim* source. *D* stands for the *Deuteronomic* source. *P* stands for the *Priestly* source. These four sources were woven together by later editors and redactors to form the present first five books of the Hebrew Torah and the Christian Old Testament.

theme involving eating the fruit from the tree of the knowledge of good and evil and the consequent banishment from the garden. Creationists refuse to accept the documentary theory and cling tenaciously to the belief in both the literal and inerrant theory of the Old and New Testaments. Randall and Buchler refer to this kind of faith as "tenacity."[5]

The theory of evolution, although not without its various and sometimes competing hypotheses, bears the weight of solid archeological, anthropological, paleontological, zoological, and biological research. Evolution is a theory. As such, it bears the weight of a preponderance of significant evidence that has not been refuted by any school of reputable scientific research.[6] Consequently, to believe in creationism is to hold a belief in spite of strong scientific evidence to the contrary. Creationists hold the steadfast belief that the scientific world of learned scholars and renowned scholarship is in serious error. To the scientific and philosophical mind, this kind of unscientific conclusion is unacceptable.

A second example of this definition of faith is in the way the Church of Rome repudiated the thinking of Galileo. Church authorities chose to scorn Galileo in spite of the evidence he proffered in support of the heliocentric hypothesis. The faith of the church fathers was a blind belief in the geocentric hypothesis in spite of evidence to the contrary.

2. Faith as belief *in the absence* of evidence to the contrary. To accept a belief because there is no evidence to the contrary is to employ negative reasoning, which claims that something is worthy of belief as long as there is no evidence against it. As such, this definition of faith is of the same fabric as the first definition. According to the second definition of faith, when there was no theory of evolution and attending hypotheses, the absence of evidence to the contrary

---

[5] Randall and Buchler, *Philosophy: An Introduction* 47.

[6] *Creationists* are quick to refer to their own body of scholarly articles purporting to disprove the theory of evolution. However, none of these articles appears in the mainstream tradition of refereed academic journals. Refereed journals rely on a process of blind peer review whereby the submitted work is circulated among at least two scholars of established academic reputation. Usually the review is a double-blind process wherein the identity of the writer(s) is obliterated from the document to be reviewed. Likewise, the identities of the reviewers are not revealed (even to each other) or published. The scholars then criticize, evaluate, and critique the submitted article and recommend for or against publication, or sometimes for publication pending revision. This blind process guarantees that the article will be accepted or rejected on the basis of merit and not because of a writer's reputation or lack of reputation. Once published, an article is then subject to peer refutation, modification, and correction, etc. The blind review is the keystone of the process of all scientific and scholarly publication, becoming common practice since the creation of specialized professions, circa 1900.

cleared the way for belief in creationism. This belief is blind faith. It is as much an exercise in tenacity as the first definition of faith, because the believer is holding a belief simply because there is a lack of significant evidence either opposed to the belief or in favor of the belief. Randall and Buchler write, "If there is evidence favoring the opinion, we ought to believe it; if the evidence is contrary to it, we ought to disbelieve; and if there is no evidence pro or con, we ought to remain in doubt. . . . (People) dislike a state of doubt. They prefer to believe something and to rest content with that belief. When they choose a belief relating to matters about which they know nothing one way or another, it will very likely be such as to fit in with their religious and ethical needs and desires."[7] Randall and Buchler refer to this second kind of faith as the will to believe.[8]

People living in the time of Copernicus or Galileo chose to scorn both of these men simply because Church authorities held that there was no convincing evidence for the heliocentric hypothesis. However, the prevailing view was wrong. Both Copernicus and Galileo did produce strong evidence in favor of the heliocentric view. The Church and its papal authority refused to accept this evidence because it threatened their favored geocentric view.

Both the first and second definitions of faith would surely not be effective in a court of law. If I had been taken to court for driving through a red light, and there was evidence from witnesses stating otherwise, convicting me would be sheer folly. But if there is an absence of testimonial and circumstantial evidence that I indeed did bring my car to a full stop, what then? To bring judgment against me without any evidence will not stand up in most courts of law. If I am to be found guilty, the evidence must point to my having run the light. You may convict me *because* of evidence, but not because of lack of evidence.

3. This brings us to our third definition of faith: faith as belief *because* of supporting evidence. Randall and Buchler refer to this kind of faith as expectation based on experience.[9] This means that I believe something to be accurate based on the evidence or on account of the evidence. This is, of course, the position of science and the sci-

---

[7] Randall and Buchler, *Philosophy: An Introduction* 48.
[8] Ibid.
[9] Ibid. 49.

entific method. Here the several theories of truth come into play: truth via the correspondence theory, the coherence theory, or a combination of both. We must always be cognizant of the possibility that what today we hold to be true may prove to be false at some future time. Nevertheless, until then, our faith is well placed if we trust the results of our hypotheses testing according to appropriate analytical procedures and statistical analyses.

In the light of scientific inquiry, let us again look at the documentary hypothesis of the authorship and construction of the five books of the Pentateuch. This hypothesis could someday be discarded. There may come a time when the theory of the J, E, D, and P strata will prove to be insufficient to answer all critical questions. New manuscripts may be discovered, as the Dead Sea Scrolls were discovered in 1947. Consequently, this hypothesis could be supplanted by another hypothesis that on examination appears to come closer to the truth of the matter.[10] The same trend of thought holds sway when we consider the ongoing and constant updating of hypotheses related to evolutionary theory. There may be changes here and there, but, to date, the overall direction and results justify our having faith in the future direction and parameters of our research.

Faith as belief because of supporting evidence is a necessary prerequisite for the advancement of knowledge. Initially, a scientist, scholar, or experimenter must have a measure of faith that a solution to his/her problem is possible, or there would be no advancement in human knowledge. Benjamin Franklin set out to establish his proposition (hypothesis) that there was an interchange of electricity between positively charged clouds and negatively charged clouds, and between clouds of one charge and objects on earth of the opposite charge. On this basis, he flew his famous kite with a key attached to the end of the string, thus establishing the hypothesis that the flow of electricity can be directed and controlled. One result of his experimentation was the invention of lightening rods. "For Franklin and his like-minded contemporaries, scientific pursuit was the ultimate act of faith; faith that there was an order to be discovered and faith in our ability to discover it."[11]

---

[10] Note that these scholars will not be using the scientific method associated with test tubes and the paraphernalia of many psychological experiments. But they will be using the lower (textual) criticism, including the rigorous comparing and analyzing of syntax, hermeneutics, grammar, writing style, and vocabulary. They will also be using the higher (historical) criticism of documents (some of which may have been previously tested using the carbon 14 test).

[11] Scott M. Leill, "Shaking the Foundation of Faith," *New York Times* Nov. 18, 2005.

So what about God? My answer is no. Your answer may be yes. In my opinion, it is entirely a question of which definition of faith one accepts as valid. If there is evidence to the contrary, then we ought to disbelieve. If there is no evidence, we ought to remain in doubt. If there is supporting evidence, then we ought to believe. Personally, I find no compelling evidence supporting the existence of a God. I find strong evidence compelling me to believe that if there is a God, this God either doesn't really give a hoot about the affairs of human beings and the lives that too many are forced to live; or that this God is a deistic force, a deus ex machina, an *élan vital*, far absent from the affairs of human existence.[12] On the other hand, I find no supporting evidence to back up a belief in either a theistic or deistic God.

In the final analysis, whether or not there is a theistic or deistic God is a matter of personal belief. As we have seen, the philosopher/scientist cannot accept the first two definitions of faith, faith *in spite of* evidence to the contrary and faith *in the absence of* evidence to the contrary. The philosopher/scientist can accept only the third definition of faith, faith *because* of supporting evidence.

What Is Left Upon Which to Build a Rational Faith?

In the absence of theism, many are tempted to find solace in deism. This is much like the eighteenth-century theologian William Paley, who waxes eloquent on the natural order and then brings God in as a last minute ringer to explain the force behind the created or natural order.[13] Paley marches in tune with a number of philosophers who simply posit a deistic force as the

---

[12] Henri Bergson; élan vital or vital force, "the vital force or impulse of life; a creative principle held by Bergson to be immanent in all organisms and responsible for evolution." *Merriam Webster's Collegiate Dictionary*.

[13] Richard Dawkins, *The Blind Watchmaker* (New York: W. W. Norton & Company, 1986). In Chapter One, Dawkins describes how Paley, in writing his *Natural Theology-Evidence of the Existence and Attributes of the Deity Collected from the Appearances of Nature* (published 1802) posits the existence of a theistic deity who is responsible for the design of the natural order much as a watchmaker is responsible for the design of a watch. Paley, living and writing before Darwin published *Origin of Species* in 1859, bases his natural theology on the order of nature and then ascribes authorship of the universe to God. Dawkins comments that before Darwin, Paley's argument carried great weight, but that since Darwin, Paley's positing of a deistic force is no longer necessary. Nevertheless, many modern Christians and Jews believe strongly that evolution best describes how the universe came into being and that the concept of God best describes the creative force behind the evolutionary process, much as Paley believed, but without benefit of Darwin's writing.

uncaused first cause in order to satisfy their desire to explain the origins of the universe.[14]

Let us take a brief look at the five arguments for the existence of God as posited by St. Thomas Aquinas. The first Thomas argument is the argument from motion. Since nothing, according to Thomas, can move on its own, there must be a prime mover. The argument comes from Aristotle. Second, since nothing in nature can be found to be the efficient cause of itself, there must be a prime cause, an uncaused first cause. Thirdy, Thomas posited the necessity of a primal source. This is the argument that there is order in the world, and, of necessity, this order is created by some being having of itself its own necessity. Argument four is the gradation argument, stating that gradation exists, such as gradation in temperature or gradation in goodness, and hence the greatest good must be God. Argument five is the teleological argument for the existence of God, an argument stating that there is purpose and design in life, and therefore there must be the ultimate director or designer.[15]

Traditionally, argument from an uncaused first cause is called the *cosmological* argument for the existence of God. Argument from order and design in nature is called the *teleological* argument. Argument from perfection in being is the *ontological* argument because it posits the necessity for the existence of perfection in being. A perfect being possesses all possible properties, including the property of its own existence.

The net result of the traditional philosophical and theological arguments for the existence of a supreme being, as portrayed by theists of differing persuasions, is failure. All of these arguments are the product of a rationalistic methodology. In the words of Randall and Buchler, "The reasoning is not supported by empirical or observational evidence but consists in deducing the consequences of principles alleged to be a priori, that is, 'self-evident' or necessarily true—for example, the principle that every series must have a first term, that order in nature presupposes an agent responsible for it, that 'absolute perfection' must exist."[16] Unfortunately, many people reason from premises they believe to be self evident and, hence, true. Nevertheless, this simply reflects their mindset of hopefulness, which then becomes the foundation stone for their faith. Recall the earlier reference to the New Testament book of Hebrews: "Now faith is the assur-

---

[14] E.g., Aristotle, Saint Anselm, Thomas Aquinas, Rene Descartes, Gottfried Leibniz, John Locke, George Berkeley, Immanuel Kant.

[15] W. T. Jones. *A History of Western Philosophy* (New York: Harcourt, Brace and Company, 1952) 445–446.

[16] Randall and Buchler, *Philosophy: An Introduction* 165 (paperback).

ance of things hoped for, the conviction of things not seen." (Hebrews 11:1 RSV) Randall and Buchler conclude, "We may reason in such a way that our conclusion determines what our reasoning shall be, or we may reason in such a way that our reasoning determines what our conclusion shall be. The latter approach alone is that of the scientific method."[17]

Many thinking people will continue to turn to Paul Tillich and his reference to the "God above the God of theism."[18] Using Tillich's spatial symbolism, this God becomes the "Ground of Being, Being Itself, Ultimate Reality," and the "Source of Being."[19] The theistic emphasis of an all-loving father who is omniscient, omnipresent, and omnipotent is absent from the implication of this new terminology. Bishop John Spong has used Tillich's terminology as the basis for a belief system that is beyond theism. Such belief and terminology, according to Spong, enables the individual to remain within a community of faith such as the church.[20] In this regard, Spong has made a valiant effort to transform the Christian Church by transcending the dogmatic tenets of Christianity.[21] In positing a God above the God of theism, Spong runs the risk of falling into a new theism, a para-theism, knowledge of which is absolutely unattainable.

Perhaps, like Spinoza of old, many today are departing from the halls of theistic and deistic thinking and are attempting to redefine the concept of God such that God is equivalent to nature and the spiritual and creative forces pervading the universe.[22] Liberal thinking people seem to be entering a time of renewed critical thinking about traditional Christianity and pietistic faith in a theistic father figure. For some, the end result is a revitalized *pantheism*, the belief that God *is* all or *panentheism*, that God is *in* all.[23] With others, it may be a spiritual consciousness or even the awe of the mystic. Erich Fromm labels the aesthetic consciousness of an expansive

---

[17] Ibid. 179.

[18] Paul Tillich, *The Courage To Be* (New Haven: Yale University Press, 1952).

[19] Ibid; (Chapter Six: *Courage and Transcendence*)

[20] John Shelby Spong, *Why Christianity Must Change or Die* (San Francisco: Harper SanFrancisco, 1998).

[21] Ibid. 225, "The experience of God as the Ground of Being has a way of breaking open every human word and making it usable again. Human language is so inadequate. All it can do is to describe human experience. Human experience can never be exhausted by language. Language can never do more than point to that which it seeks to describe. It can never capture truth."

[22] Jonathan Bennett, "Glimpses of Spinoza," *The Syracuse Scholar* (Spring 1983) 43-56.

[23] http://websyte.com/alan/pan.htm. Also see Spong, *Why Christianity* 62.

universe the *x* experience.[24] John Dewey spoke about the religious *attitude* as being the essence of "*A Common Faith*," rather than specific religious practices, dogmas, and organizations.[25]

The title of this chapter asks the question, "Is there really God?" The answer to that question can never be known. The reason the answer can never be known is that the word *really* implies *in reality*. In reality, is there a single theistic God? Perhaps yes. Perhaps no. In either case, the ultimate reality is beyond the limit and capacity of human knowledge and human reason. If the question were to be put a different way—e.g., "Is there God?"—the answer would be that there are conceivably as many Gods as there are human minds involved in the constructive creation of these Gods.

This brings us back to the main theme of these pages—constructivism. Gods exist by courtesy of the minds that invent, create, and fashion them. As was emphasized in the previous chapter on truth, each one of us may have a first order truth concerning our belief about the existence of God. Whatever that belief is or is not, it constitutes our belief or nonbelief, our faith or nonfaith. Second-order truth, the truth about what constitutes ultimate reality, must remain forever beyond the capacity of the human mind to comprehend. Like second-order truth, second-order reality is beyond the ken of human existence. While we can talk about it and speculate about it, we cannot *know* it in any final, meaningful, and ordinary sense of the word.

---

[24] Erich Fromm, "The Concept of God," from *You Shall Be As Gods*. (New York: Holt, Rinehart and Winston, 1966) For an excellent analysis of the evolution of rational religious belief, see Fromm, *The Art of Loving* (New York: Harper & Row, 1956),Chapter II, Section 3e, "Love of God," 63-82.

[25] Dewey, John, *A Common Faith* New Haven: Yale University Press, 1934.

Chapter Five

The Anatomy of Theistic Belief

WHAT ARE the driving factors in causing people to believe the things they believe? We have considered the "what?" and the "how do we know?" of belief, but what about the "why?" of belief? Why do humans believe the things they do?

Sam Harris comments: "Although many things can be said in criticism of religious faith, there is no discounting its power. Millions among us, even now, are quite willing to die for our unjustified beliefs, and millions more, it seems, are willing to kill for them. Those who are destined to suffer terribly throughout their lives, or upon the threshold of death, often find consolation in one unfounded proposition or another. Faith enables many of us to endure life's difficulties with an equanimity that would be scarcely conceivable in a world lit only by reason."[1]

In order to cut this question down to a manageable size, our concern will be limited to *theistic* belief.[2] In short, we are not embarking on an overall study of the psychology of religious belief or the philosophy of religious belief. Our issue is one of traditional monotheism, wherein the deity is conceptualized as a transcendent, omnipotent, omniscient being as well as an immanent force directing the daily affairs of individuals and nations. What are the motivating factors that lead people to this basic belief? By way of answer I shall first turn to the work of Abraham Maslow.[3]

---

[1] Sam Harris, *The End of Faith: Religion, Terror, and the Future of Reason* (New York: W.W. Norton, 2004) 64.

[2] According to a *Newsweek* poll from December 2004, 94% of Americans claim they believe in God. December, 2004.

[3] Abraham Maslow, "A Theory of Human Motivation," *Psychological Review* 50 (1943) 370–396.

THE FLIPSIDE OF GODSPEAK

Abraham Maslow and Prepotent Need Theory

Psychologist Abraham Maslow created a theory of basic human needs with each need being prepotent over lower needs. Maslow's most pressing basic human needs are called "deficiency" or "D" needs, because whenever a deficiency need is experienced the human organism will act to meet this need, at least to the point where the person can function. Maslow outlines four deficiency needs that are prepotent in nature—that is, they are basic needs that must be met before a person seeks to fill less urgent needs. The higher or more elementary the need, the stronger its power, force, or influence in motivating the individual to action. According to Maslow, the hierarchy of "D" needs is (1) physical needs, such as food, drink, sleep, warmth;(2) needs for psychological and physical safety; (3) the need to be loved or the need for love; and (4) the need for esteem, both self esteem and the esteem of others.

A person may be functioning fairly well in meeting all of these "D" needs, but if this person happened to be at the seashore when suddenly a tsunami crashed ashore, the person would quickly regress to prepotent physical and safety needs. This means that no matter what the person was doing, nothing now is as important as reaching physical safety. In Maslow's hierarchy of needs, each of the "D" needs must receive some degree of satisfaction before a person is free to move downward to the next lower need in the hierarchy of needs. Any level may collapse at any time because of specific circumstances and crises. Thus, if a dating couple riding in a car together, seemingly occupied with expressions of mutual affection, is suddenly confronted with the flashing lights of police cars and ambulances on the road ahead, they both will likely quickly regress to the level of physical safety, even if only for a short time. This means that until they feel safe they will not be motivated by any other need.

Once a human has her/his four basic "D" needs met, at least to a satisfactory minimal point, Maslow's second category of needs comes into play, called "being" or "B" needs. Being needs are ongoing and they are not prepotent. Being needs include the human quest for truth, beauty, justice, equality, fairness, respect, kindness, honesty, self-responsibility, and all other aesthetic and personal/character type needs.

The Second Deficiency Need: Physical Safety and Psychological Safety

I hold that the anatomy of theistic belief is almost entirely rooted in physical and psychological or emotional (psycho-emotional) security. I say "almost," because there are times when we may be physically safe yet in desperate need of food, clothing and shelter, which are prepotent over physical safety. (Imagine you are stranded in a lifeboat and you definitely are *not* physically or emotionally safe, yet the need for food and warm clothing is overwhelming and all possessing.)

The operative question for most human beings is how to manage the higher anxiety levels that result from deficits (or perceived deficits) in Maslow's hierarchy of "D" needs. In order to address this question, we must consider how anxiety becomes bound, i.e., how it is managed so that it is less painful and bothersome.

The Binding of Anxiety

The binding of anxiety constitutes a manner of belief and/or behavior that tends to reduce our anxiety and make ourselves feel more calm and collected, more in control, and less bothered with worry and fear. We bind our anxiety in myriads of ways, many of them very obscure and even unconscious. Obvious binders are illicit drugs, alcohol, sex (including ongoing marital sex), participatory sports, spectator sports, behavioral rituals such as frequent bathing, frequent snacking, overeating, undereating, and even talking. Less obvious binders include obsessive-compulsive behaviors such as frequent checking of the stove, the water faucets, and the lights in the basement. Kerr and Bowen state: "Relationships are by far the most effective anxiety binders. . . . People who deny their need for attachment to others are just as relationship-dependent as those who constantly seek a relationship. Loners can bind just as much anxiety by avoiding people as people who constantly seek social contact can bind anxiety through that contact."[4]

Let us be clear that the human emotion of fear is not identical with anxiety. Most of the time we can relate fear to a specific object. Usually, anxiety is much more difficult to pinpoint than fear. Anxiety is usually a reflection of something that presents as vague and objectless. Psychologists

---

[4] Michael E. Kerr and Murray Bowen, *Family Evaluation: An Approached Based on Bowen Theory* (New York: W.W. Norton and Company, 1998) 119.

and psychiatrists often refer to anxiety as "free floating," i.e., it has no identifiable object, and it attaches itself to many various activities and behaviors.[5]

Suffice it to say that the binding of anxiety is universal. It is a trait shared by all human beings. People of low angst are indeed fortunate, but even they have to do something with their anxiety. It is axiomatic that those with high levels of anxiety will go to great lengths to achieve some degree of calmness and inner peace. In order to accomplish this, we learn to bind our anxiety, albeit on a subconscious level.

Beliefs and the Binding of Anxiety

Kerr and Bowen state: "Beliefs are an especially important anxiety binder... The inclination to 'see' the world as other than it really is—more as one imagines, wishes, or fears it to be—is a pretty compelling force in everyone.... People who join cults and adopt the belief system of the cult increase their feeling of emotional well-being and function better. The number of people who make important life decisions based on astrological predictions is testimony to the power of beliefs for reducing anxiety.... Most people have at least some degree of emotional investment in what they believe, and a threat to the validity of the belief creates some distress."[6]

Combining the concept of "D" needs with the concept of the binding of anxiety results in the following proposition: Specific beliefs about the existence and character of a theistic God serve as a major construct enabling humans to cope with the vicissitudes of life. This constructed belief in a theistic deity is perhaps the most significant step a person can take toward meeting his/her need for psycho-emotional safety, the second highest motivational need on Maslow's "D" need hierarchy.

My thesis throughout this chapter is that the *chief* reason (there are others) people choose to believe in a theistic God is because this belief gives them a sense of psycho-emotional security that they have not found anywhere else in life. In other words, people believe what they need to believe in order to survive, cope with life, and keep their level of anxiety under control. The greater one's anxiety, the more prepotent the need to allay the discomfort of insecurity. The need to feel psychologically safe is a continu-

---

[5] John F. Crosby, "Theories of Anxiety: A Theoretical Perspective," *The American Journal of Psychoanalysis* 36, 3, (1976).

[6] Kerr and Bowen, *Family Evaluation* 120–121

ing deficiency need, sometimes more acute and sometimes less acute, but always playing a prominent role in the functioning of the individual.

What Specific Needs are Included in Psycho-Emotional Security?

The need to believe in a theistic God is varied and diverse. It manifests itself in many different ways. Following is a brief description of several manifestations of the basic need to believe. The list is certainly not exhaustive or all-inclusive.

- *The need to rid oneself of fear of death and the unknown.* A cursory reading of the history of the monotheistic religions of the world reveals that by far the most popular and widespread antidote to the primal fear of death and the unknown is theistic belief.[7] Such belief stems the tide and calms the restlessness of the soul, even as it hides from our consciousness the simple fact that none of us has any verifiable knowledge of what happens to us the moment life passes from our body.

- *The need to ameliorate the fear of punishment.* This is related to the preceding need, but it is a far more powerful fear for some, depending on what teachings about eternal punishment were internalized. Fear of punishment ranges from visions of a burning inferno to drowning and torture of all descriptions.

- *The need to be relieved of feelings of guilt and shame.* Feelings of an all-pervasive personal guilt and sense of personal shame, however irrational they may be, tend to take hold of how a person feels about himself/herself. This in turn has an undue influence on one's sense of self or self-image.

- *The need for forgiveness, reconciliation, and atonement.* Many people have so completely and thoroughly internalized their own sense of guilt and failure over their self-conviction of having fallen short of the demands of a theistic deity that they hunger for a feeling of

---

[7] See Sigmund Freud, *The Future of An Illusion* (New York:Anchor Books, Doubleday & Company, 1927); Karen Armstrong, *A History of God: The 4,000 Year Quest of Judaism, Christianity and Islam* (New York: Alfred A. Knopf, 1994); and R. B. Stewart Jr., *On the Origin of Gods* (Powell, Tenn.: Powell Publishing, 2004).

having been forgiven. This sense of being forgiven paves the way for reconciliation and a sense of being *at-one* (at-one-ment) with the Godhead.

- *The need to be "saved" or "born again" into a state of sinlessness and perfection.* This need is part of the previous four, but it is clothed in a language arising from the evangelical and fundamentalist acceptance of the penal-substitutionary theory of the atonement. This entails the belief that God willed the death of Jesus in order to serve as the payment (expiation) for human sin, i.e., that Jesus took upon himself the punishment humans deserve.

- *The need to be delivered from a sense of despair.* Ernest Becker states: "It was not until the working out of modern psychoanalysis that we could understand something the poets and religious geniuses have long known: that the armor of character was so vital to us that to shed it meant to risk death and madness. It is not hard to reason out: If character is a neurotic defense against despair, and you shed that defense, you admit the full flood of despair, the full realization of the true human condition, what men are really afraid of, what they struggle against, and are driven toward and away from."[8] Despair is related to anxiety, and it usually indicates a sense of being frantic and disillusioned, a sense of hopelessness and dread.

- *The need to have an identity that is anchored in a divine being.* For Christians, this may be similar to St. Paul's "For me to live is Christ." (Philippians 1:21) and "I live, yet not I, but Christ liveth in me." (Galatians 2:20) For non-Christian theists, this identity may be characterized as a fusion or an enmeshment into the divine being.

- *The need for comfort and mental peace.* When people lose loved ones to death, it can be very comforting to believe that one day there will be a reunion. This belief often manifests itself most powerfully when a child, teenager, or young adult precedes the parents in death. The belief that one will be reunited with husband, wife, mother, father, son, or daughter is frequently the strongest motivating force in the practice of one's beliefs.

---

[8] Becker, *Denial of Death* 56–57.

- *The need for a sense of purpose and meaning in life.* Countless numbers of people defend against the anxiety of a perceived meaningless and purposelessness in life by believing that God has a specific purpose for them. Some hold to a belief that God has a specific plan for everyone, including what one is to do with one's life, whom to marry, and what to do in specific conflicted situations. (Chapter Eight will treat the issue of purpose and meaning in greater detail.)

In each of the above illustrations, the belief in a theistic God will contribute significantly to the binding of anxiety. The rewards for belief can be many. Each of the rewards or benefits contributes to the sense of psychological safety, the second of Maslow's "D" needs. It is important that we not underestimate how these beliefs enable millions of believers to cope with frightening and powerful vicissitudes in the pilgrimage of life.

Freud, Becker, and Tillich on the Why of Belief

Freud's *The Future of an Illusion* is still very much a work that is relevant for the twenty-first century. According to Freud, the reason for belief, i.e., the 'why' of belief, is the early predicament of the human infant/child. The child is first protected by the loving mother, who cuddles the infant in the warmth of her flowing breast. Soon, however, the child learns that the father is the one who really is his/her protector. This situation then transforms into a scenario wherein the child is beholden to the father for protection and at the same time learns to fear the father because the father has the power to give approval and disapproval, probation and approbation. Freud states:

> When the growing individual finds that he is destined to remain a child for ever, that he can never do without protection against strange superior powers, he lends those powers the features belonging to the figure of his father; he creates for himself the gods whom he dreads, whom he seeks to propitiate, and whom he nevertheless entrusts with his own protection. Thus his longing for a father is a motive identical with his need for protection against the consequences of his human weakness.[9]

Enter the societal and cultural belief system, the system of legends and myths, traditions and customs, and the child will grow up believing that

---

[9] Freud, *Future of Illusion* 35.

THE FLIPSIDE OF GODSPEAK

the father of his/her childhood has mutated into the godhead of religious belief. The father of infant protection and fear has become the father of humankind, replete with the ability to protect against human transgressors as well as the insults and ravages of nature. Freud states:

> And thus a store of ideas is created, born from man's need to make his helplessness tolerable and built up from the material of memories of the helplessness of his own childhood and the childhood of the human race. It can clearly be seen that the possession of these ideas protects him in two directions—against the dangers of nature and Fate, and against the injuries that threaten him from human society itself. . . . I have tried to show that religious ideas have arisen from the same need as have all the other achievements of civilization: from the necessity of defending oneself against the crushingly superior force of nature.[10]

For Freud, a wish is parent to the illusion. "They are illusions, fulfilments (sic) of the oldest, strongest and most urgent wishes of mankind. The secret of their strength lies in the strength of those wishes."[11]

Freud uses the word *protection,* and I have used Maslow's words, *psychological safety.* Since Freud's protection includes the ravages of nature and physical survival, we should also emphasize Maslow's dual emphasis on physical and psychological safety.

Clearly, not only does humankind construct the deity that it worships, it also turns to various other beliefs and behaviors that tend to bring temporary relief to anxiety, despair, and a sense of futility and meaninglessness. Ernest Becker points out in his seminal work, *The Denial of Death*:

> All of us are driven to be supported in a self-forgetful way, ignorant of what energies we really draw on, of the kind of *lie* we have fashioned in order to live securely and serenely. Augustine was a master analyst of this, as were Kierkegaard, Scheler, and Tillich in our day. They saw that man could strut and boast all he wanted, but that he really drew his 'courage to be' from a god, a string of sexual conquests, a Big Brother, a flag, the proletariat, and the fetish of money and the size of a bank balance."[12] (Italics added)

Becker demonstrates the extent to which humans attempt to lie to themselves, kid themselves, fool themselves, and otherwise deceive themselves through various escape and defense mechanisms. Becker's work is

---

[10] Ibid. 23–24; 30.
[11] Ibid. 47.
[12] Becker, *Denial of Death* 55–56.

a testimonial to the stubbornness with which human beings deny the reality of death. Becker claims that no matter how we seek to deny it or escape from it, the repression of death, an ongoing unconscious behavior, serves to protect us from the ultimate anxiety. In a direct contradiction of Freud, Becker says, "Consciousness of death is the primary repression, not sexuality."[13]

Tillich, in his insightful contribution to the literature of psychology and religion, *The Courage To Be*, identifies the fundamental human problem as learning to live with anxiety.[14]

> It is the anxiety of not being able to preserve one's own being which underlies every fear and is the frightening element in it. In the moment, therefore, in which "naked anxiety" lays hold of the mind, the previous objects of fear cease to be definite objects. They appear as what they always were in part, symptoms of man's basic anxiety. As such they are beyond the reach of even the most courageous attack upon them. This situation drives the anxious subject to establish objects of fear. Anxiety strives to become fear, because fear can be met by courage. It is impossible for a finite being to stand naked anxiety for more than a flash of time.[15]

According to Tillich, the human dilemma is how to rid oneself of this most basic anxiety, i.e., how to preserve one's own being. Courage may succeed against fear, but it will not succeed against the most basic anxiety. It is at this point that Tillich changes the focus of courage from an attack upon anxiety itself to the ongoing effort to weave this anxiety into the fabric of one's own being.

> Courage does not remove anxiety. Since anxiety is existential, it cannot be removed. But courage takes the anxiety of nonbeing into itself. Courage is self-affirmation "in spite of," namely in spite of nonbeing. He who acts courageously takes, in his self-affirmation, the anxiety of non-being upon himself."[16]

At the beginning of this chapter we asked, "What are the driving factors in causing people to believe the things they believe?" There are several forces clustered around the central theme of anxiety. We began with the second-highest prepotent "D" need in Maslow's hierarchy, *physical and psychological safety*. Then we considered the phenomenon known as the *binding*

---

[13] Ibid. 96.
[14] Tillich. *The Courage To Be*.
[15] Ibid. 38-39 (1952 paperback edition).
[16] Ibid; 66

of anxiety and how this tends to make us feel better in the face of personal and cosmic insecurity. According to Freud, the individual uses religion and belief in God as *protection* against the onslaught of both natural and societal forces. Becker sees *repression* of the consciousness of death as the most powerful means by which humankind copes with the anxiety of death, using God, religion, sex, money, and even patriotism as defenses against the inevitable. Finally, Tillich, instead of seeking to "bind" the basic ontological anxiety, seeks to incorporate it into one's selfhood. This is his *courage to be*.

The inevitable conclusion is that the human need for physical and psycho-emotional safety, including deliverance and escape from the most threatening form of anxiety, the anxiety of meaninglessness, nonbeing, and nothingness is the driving force behind theistic belief.

Beliefs in Transition

There can be little question that Charles Darwin's publication of *The Origin of Species* in 1859 marked the beginning of a transition from the age of theistic belief to what has come to be known as the post-Christian era. If we were able to observe from some far distant time and place, we might be able to see clearly that the pre-Darwin theological perspective began to crumble, however slowly, with the growing acceptance of natural selection. The liberal wings of Reform Judaism, Islam, and Christianity, usually reviled by the more conservative branches and constituencies within the same persuasions, made a bold effort to hold to theism by positing the deity at the apex of natural selection. For these liberal believers, God was held to be the "why" of creation, and natural selection is held to be the "how" of creation. This worked well for the second and third quarters of the twentieth century, but slowly and with painstaking agony the theological house of cards began to crumble.

No one can prognosticate with any real authority. However, since humankind has been inventing gods for well over 4,000 years—i.e., in biblical history at least since Abraham, circa 1900 BCE—it seems reasonable that at least half as long a time—i.e., 2,000 years—could be necessary for the vast majority of inhabitants of the world to outgrow the need for theistic belief.

Of course, there will always be those who believe. They *need* to believe. They *wish* to believe. They *want* to believe. And they *will* to believe. As time goes by, the pendulum of belief vs. unbelief and faith vs. nonfaith is likely to swing many times between periods of stable tranquility and periods of anxiety. Perhaps humankind will never be able to bear the anxiety of waiting without idols and will continue to take solace in some form of theism in order to bind the anxiety of death and nothingness. Nevertheless, I remain hopeful that the paradigm will shift to a point where a small yet significant minority will have persuasive dominance over the vociferous minions of evangelical believers and literalistic fundamentalists.[17]

---

[17] Thomas S. Kuhn, *The Structure of Scientific Revolutions* (Chicago: The University of Chicago Press, 1962).

Chapter Six

Can There Be Morality without God? I: Authority in Ethics

I DESCRIBED MY beliefs about god, theism, atheism, and agnosticism to a married man with whom I was having a serious discussion. He said to me, "If I believed as you do, I would be chasing women with but one goal in mind." Of course, I could not resist asking him why. He replied, "If there is no God, anything goes. If there is no God, there is no punishment."

In a similar vein, a mature female acquaintance alleged that she didn't have much opinion one way or the other about the existence of God, but that the Church was important to her because this is where her children learned morality. "Belief in God," she alleged, "is the source of moral and ethical behavior." Upon further questioning, she volunteered that she believed children must be taught to be afraid of punishment, for if they did not learn to fear authority, they would grow up without any sense of morality.

Any serious discussion about ethics and morality must address itself to certain basic questions. Why are there sufficient food and resources on our planet to feed a population of six billion, and yet in many parts of the world there is starvation and death due to the diseases that result from poor diet? Why are some 90 percent of the financial resources of the planet controlled by the top two or three percent of the population? Why do governments prevent the spread of knowledge and materials necessary for the prevention of unwanted pregnancy and AIDS? Why do some governments deny abortion even to the victims of rape and incest on the grounds that the will of God or Allah is opposed to such measures? In other words, in the name of God or Allah, we participate in planetary hunger and starvation, sexually transmitted disease patterns, compulsory pregnancy even for victims of rape and incest, child labor and child slavery, and pollution of the environment. As Sam Harris observes, "The pervasive idea that religion is somehow the source of our deepest ethical intuitions is absurd."[1]

Authoritarian and Humanistic Ethics

Through the ages there have been many authoritarian systems of ethical principles and injunctions that both prescribe and proscribe human behavior. These include, among many others, the Code of Hammurabi, the Jewish Torah, the Christian Bible, and the Islamic Koran. Except for the Code of Hammurabi, they are labeled authoritarian because the foundation of each system is alleged to be either divine or supernatural in some sense, and as such there is an irrational claim to validity, credibility, and veracity. The Code of Hammurabi was based on still older codes of law, and tradition holds that the sun god Shamash, the patron of justice, was the divine symbol of Babylonian authority.[2]

Erich Fromm points out that authority is not necessarily a negative characteristic.[3] The alternative to dictatorial irrational authority need not be the absence of authority. The question that begs to be asked is what kind of authority, irrational or rational? While irrational authority abounds throughout history, rational authority is a necessary basis for the social order and the social compact form of civil government. Rational authority underlies all intellectual and scientific endeavors insofar as the person, persons, or collective political entities in positions of authority retain that authority by reason of training, education, or public endorsement. As Fromm states: "Rational authority has its source in competence. The person whose authority is respected functions competently in the task with which he is entrusted by those who conferred it upon him. He need not intimidate them nor arouse their admiration by magic qualities; as long as and to the extent to which he is competently helping, instead of exploiting, his authority is based on rational grounds and does not call for irrational awe. . . . The source of *irrational authoriy* . . . is always power *over* people."[4]

---

[1] Sam Harris, *The End of Faith* (New York: W. W. Norton & Company, 2004) 171.

[2] The Tao Te Ching of Lao Tsu is not really an authoritative code in the manner of the Torah or Koran. It is, however, a highly revered and respected source of wisdom in matters both practical and aesthetic.

[3] Erich Fromm, "Chapter Two, Section One: Humanistic vs. Authoritarian Ethics," in *Man For Himself* (New York: Holt, Rinehart, and Winston, 1947).

[4] Ibid.

A humanistic ethic is always based on rational authority. Rational authority does not wield power over people unless at the behest of a consensus on the part of the electorate. Rational authority has its roots, as Fromm says, in competence and in the judicious use of legitimate power. This principle applies whether in a democracy or in a university classroom, where the professor, by virtue of training, education, and experience, is considered to have authority within the bounds of his/her field of expertise.

Sources of Authority in Ethical Matters

There are several sources or grounds for ethics. One is simply common sense, which in popular usage refers to basic intelligence about practical matters.[5] When we say that someone has a lot of common sense, we are usually paying that person a compliment. We are saying she/he displays sound and solid judgment about everyday things. Common sense can also mean beliefs that appear to be common to all people, i.e., sense in common, based on strong consensus. We spoke in Chapter Three about truth being sometimes based on consensus of opinion or belief. Unfortunately, common sense referred to in the consensual definition of truth is often held to be authoritative, especially in matters of religion, politics, and advertising. (Ninety-four percent of Americans believe in God. The Ten Commandments should be prominently displayed in schools and in courthouses. A majority of dentists recommend Whito-Brito tooth paste as being best. According to the voluptuous looking blonde, Burpo Beer is less filling.) The use of common sense as a legitimate source of authority, as with the question of truth, simply falls short of the mark. At times it may appear to be rational and at other times irrational. At best it is unreliable, and at worst it is false and misleading.

Faith as a source of authority and knowledge was discussed in Chapter Four. Suffice it to say that the same objections highlighted in the discussion of knowledge about the existence of God or gods apply to the issue of authority. When faith is used as the basis of authority, does the individual believe in spite of evidence to the contrary, in the absence of evidence to the contrary, or because of evidence in support? Only in the last of these three definitions can faith be a legitimate source of authority.

A third popular source of authority is intuition. This is an extremely individualistic view of authority and one that is probably responsible for a

---

[5] *Merriam-Webster's Collegiate Dictionary*, Eleventh Edition, 2003: "sound and prudent judgment based on a simple perception of the situation or facts."

great deal of good in human life, as well as a great deal of evil. If my intuitive sense tells me that I had better check on my neighbor because he is elderly and I haven't seen him around for several days, and it turns out that, indeed, he was in dire straits, then my intuition proved helpful. This is an example of intuition based on two facts, my neighbor is elderly and I have not seen him around for several days. However, if my intuition convinces the president of the United States (and hundreds of thousands of others) that a rogue dictator needs to be taken down, that intuition is indeed suspect as a legitimate source of authority. At best, intuition is subject to inner streams of consciousness. At worst, it gives sway to our deepest wishes and fears, which often become the progenitors of untold evil. In the name of intuition, innocent people have been maligned and stripped of their basic rights.

Dogma and tradition are also types of authority. Both are promulgated by religious and state/political institutions, and both tend to discourage independent thinking. Randall and Buchler remind us:

> The man who is primarily interested in preserving his beliefs is not likely to be the kind of man who has arrived at them in an independent way. Even those who are most willing to discard untenable opinions cannot escape the pervasive influence of authority. The family, the legal code, the state, the church, social custom, and the printed page—all function as authorities propagating opinions that cannot be wholly avoided even by the most critical. In some cases, as for instance the family and the social mores, beliefs are assimilated unconsciously. In other cases, as for instance the state and the church, the authority is consciously looked up to, and deliberately functions as an agency that legislates on truth and falsity, and on desirability and undesirability of belief."[6]

The method of basing knowledge and the quest for truth upon the alleged authority of state/political and religious institutions is tantamount to abdicating one's own responsibility. Seeking and working through the deepest and most important issues and problems one encounters in life, painstaking and difficult as it may be, is the only legitimate substitute for the blind acceptance of authority.

---

[6] John Herman Randall Jr. and Justus Buchler, "Chapter Five," in *Philosophy: An Introduction* (New York: Barnes and Noble, 1942).

The Ten Commandments

The Ten Commandments amount to little more than prescriptions and proscriptions that a tribal and localized God has supposedly imposed on a nomadic, wandering people. As such, the commandments have enjoyed observance more in the breach than in obedience. With respect to adultery, at the historical point in time that the decalogue was believed to have been written, the Jewish male was permitted to copulate with any woman other than a Jewess. He could have sexual intercourse with a slave woman, a Canaanite, a Philistine, or any woman captured in war and would not be committing adultery. Further, God was depicted as a jealous god who did not permit graven images. In addition, the prohibitions against stealing and coveting were more observed in the breaking than in the keeping. Certainly the commandment against killing had little clout, because killing was rampant throughout the Hebrew Bible. In short, laws prohibiting killing, stealing, and coveting were violated regularly in dealings with outsiders. John Spong says, "A careful study of these codes reveals nothing less than the tribal prejudices, stereotypes, and limited knowledge of the people who created them."[7] As an ethical ideal for modern thinking people, the commandments have little to recommend them, simply because they weren't followed.

The Scientific Method

Each of the foregoing sources of authority stands in sharp contrast to the methodology and procedures of the scientific method of inquiry. In its most broad applications, the scientific method and the spirit of empirical investigation can be applied to a great diversity of subjects, including history, literature, and the arts.

We frequently associate the scientific method with the so-called hard sciences, but increasingly, research within the social sciences is guided by hypothesis testing and empirical inquiry. At a basic statistical level, the hypothesized or expected frequency of occurrence of an event can be computed against actual observed occurrence, be it literary or scientific. If an event can be counted, it can be tested against the frequency of occurrences.

Hypothesis testing utilizing both the higher and lower criticisms is applicable to many issues in literature, ancient and modern. In addition to

---

[7] John Shelby Spong, *Why Christianity Must Change Or Die*. San Francisco: Harper SanFrancisco, 1998) 151. For a more complete analysis of the tribal prohibitions and injunctions see 150–155, 159, 208.

the Koran and the Bible, it is applicable to the Vedas and the Upanishads, as well as to Chaucer, Shakespeare, and Tolstoy. Hypothesis testing is applicable to economics, engineering, pharmacology, medicine, anthropology, geology, archeology, paleontology, child development, personality development, and life-cycle development.

As Fromm suggests, rational authority is based on the competence of those who by reason of education, training, experience, or public endorsement are elected or appointed to positions of influence and power.[8] One outstanding characteristic of rational authority is its basic premise that allows for the ever-present possibility of error. In the light of new knowledge and new research, old hypotheses and theories need to be revisited. In contrast to irrational authority, rational authority flourishes on the principle that there is no absolute dictum that is beyond reconsideration in the light of new evidence.

Because rational authority is always cognizant of the possibility of error and is therefore not foolproof, many people flee to the security of dictums of faith as promulgated by church, synagogue, or mosque. The main thesis of Erich Fromm's seminal work, *Escape From Freedom*, is that people who demand the security of final answers and codified truth will turn their backs on freedom in order to worship at the shrine of emotional and psychological security.[9] The appeal to authority, be it in the form of gods, bibles, or political pronouncements, tends to help people feel secure and safe. Submission to irrational authority binds one's anxiety and relieves one of feelings of being lost, being helpless, and being adrift without anchor. Some people have yet to learn that the price of freedom is insecurity and that the price of security is the loss of personal freedom.

Of this we can be certain. Whatever authority is posited as being rational, just, equitable, blind to religious preference, blind to color, blind to gender and sex identity, blind to ethnicity, and blind to privilege must be subject to continual critical debate and evaluation. Ongoing scrutiny in the spirit of scientific methodology must be the order of the day. Appeal to authority must, of necessity, be a rational appeal, or it is nothing more than the perpetuation of tyranny.

---

[8] Fromm, "Chapter Two, Section 1, Humanistic vs. Authoritarian Ethics," in *Man for Himself*.

[9] Erich Fromm. *Escape From Freedom*. (New York: Holt, Rinehart & Winston, 1941).

Chapter Seven

Can There Be Morality without God? II: An Ethic of Well-being

Kohlberg's Theory of Moral Development

AMONG ALL the lines of inquiry by educators, early-childhood researchers, family researchers, social workers, psychologists, and psychiatrists into the question of how we learn to be moral, one researcher stands out as a pioneer. Lawrence Kohlberg's work gained national and international attention in the early 1970s. Kohlberg is a developmental psychologist who was strongly influenced by Jean Piaget. Kohlberg's research underlies a set of hypotheses that continues to command research attention. Certainly Kohlberg is not to be thought of as having any final answers. But he is to be recognized for the fact that his work opened up a field of inquiry that had hitherto been neglected.

Kohlberg posits three levels of moral development, with two stages for each level.[1] The three levels—preconventional, conventional, and postconventional—give some clue to the direction and nature of Kohlberg's thinking. But it is the description and characterization of each of the six stages that guide the research endeavor.

- Level I, Preconventional
    Stage 1. Obedience and Punishment
    Stage 2. Reward and Social Exchange

---

[1] Lawrence Kohlberg, *The Philosophy of Moral Development* (New York: Harper & Row, 1981).

- Level II, Conventional
    Stage 3. Good Boy/Girl
    Stage 4. Law and Order/Conformity

- Level III, Postconventional
    Stage 5. Social Contract
    Stage 6. Principled Conscience

The preconventional level, (usually kindergarten and elementary school) consists of stages 1 and 2, generally characterized as obedience and threat of punishment, and is the most elemental of the stages. Everyone begins here. The threat of punishment is the effective motivator, and children learn to obey in order to avoid punishment as well as to please the parental authorities. Stage 2, reward and social exchange, brings in the positive side of obedience, in that the reward for not being disobedient is parental approval. The exchange is twofold: If I am good, I will not be punished. If I am good, it will please Mommy and/or Daddy. At this stage, acceptable behavior is acting in one's own best interest.

The conventional level consists of stages 3 and 4. In the good boy/girl stage, the emphasis is on conformity in order to avoid disapproval and to gain approval. Children learn quickly that certain social behaviors with other children bring rewards of acceptance and affirmation, while other activities, such as hostility, aggression, and demeaning behavior, often serve to distance and alienate potential friends. Stage 4, law and order, stresses a sense of duty and conformity to avoid censure by authorities. Here, the welfare of others and the greater good of society are important.

Level three, postconventional, consists of stages 5 and 6. Stage 5, a social contract, involves the acceptance of democratic law and a focus on the rule of law for community welfare. The emphasis is on social reciprocity and a concern for the welfare of others. Stage 6, principled conscience, emphasizes individual, community, and universal ethical principles and abstract ideals.

Kohlberg later relented on stage 6, saying that it was an ideal stage that no one ever really attained. It is important to view Kohlberg's system as one in which steps cannot be skipped. We learn as we grow. In Piaget's terminology, assimilation is followed by accommodation whenever new ideas, thoughts, or behaviors enter the picture, and most of the learning is done within a context of social interaction.

The most telling feature of Kohlberg's classification is the striking fact that huge numbers of people never grow beyond stage 2. Kohlberg believed that only a minority of people ever grow beyond stage 4. Stage 5 is more likely to be manifest in democratic rather than authoritarian societies. Kohlberg claimed his system applied to all cultures and societies. This is a questionable assumption because so much of social learning is the result of the socialization process peculiar to any given society and its cultural and religious teachings.

The Golden Rule in Kohlberg's System

The Golden Rule, known as such only since the eighteenth century, is variously thought to be of Judean, pagan, or Christian origin.[2] This injunction raises questions as to motivation. Does it veil a calculating egoism? Does it imply one should not go beyond self-interest? Does it make oneself the single standard of proper treatment of others rather than the other person's welfare? When the Golden Rule is placed into Kohlberg's taxonomy, it would be difficult to place it higher than stage four. This is conventional moral behavior, with its emphasis on law, order, a sense of duty, and avoidance of censure by authorities. If the Golden Rule had a universal referent rather than a self-referent (based on the well-being of others rather than on oneself), it could be elevated to postconventional stage five moral behavior, i.e., principled on a sense of altruism and the welfare of humankind. However, as it stands, in either its negative or positive form, it is a rule that is based on self-centeredness.

Criticism and Evaluation of Kohlberg

Unfortunately, Kohlberg's research was based entirely on males. Carol Gilligan[3] provides an alternate perspective on Kohlberg's work. Gilligan questioned whether females go through the same sequence of stages as males, especially since girls are more likely to be socialized into the im-

---

[2] The Golden Rule is part of Jesus' sermon on the mount (Matthew: 7:12) and sermon on the plain (Luke 6:31). The Golden Rule is also to be found in negative form in the Tobit 4:15, "What you hate, don't do to someone else." Tradition claims that Jesus first cast the rule into its positive form: "Do unto others as you would have others do unto you." Rabbi Hillel, a Judean contemporary of Jesus, is credited with saying: "What you hate, don't do to another. That's the law in a nutshell; everything else is commentary." According to the Jesus Seminar, it is unlikely that these are authentic words of Jesus. Robert W. Funk and Roy W. Hoover, and the Jesus Seminar, *The Five Gospels: What Did Jesus Really Say?* (New York: Macmillan Publishing Company, Polebridge Press, 1993) 156, 296.

[3] Carol Gilligan, *In A Different Voice: Psychological Theory and Women's Development* (Cambridge, Mass.: Harvard University Press, 1982).

portance of maintaining relationships rather than striving for moral justice, individuation, and achievement. Gilligan states: "Only when life-cycle theorists divide their attention and begin to live with women as they have lived with men will their vision encompass the experience of both sexes and their theories become correspondingly more fertile."[4] Research in human development is increasingly coming to understand and allow for the fact that males and females are frequently socialized differently and are taught to reason and think within the framework of a different set of parameters.

Nevertheless, my main theme here is neither to defend nor attack Kohlberg. My concern is to highlight an entire field of ethical-moral research that attempts to show that both men and women begin to develop their sense of morals at a rudimentary level of fear of punishment, the importance of obedience, and the quest for reward. Whether or not subsequent research will confirm Kohlberg's hypotheses remains to be seen. Certainly there is much to endorse in Gilligan's criticism. Nevertheless, what is well established is the proposition that morality and moral-ethical thinking is the result of early socialization and peer interaction with one's own sex as well as the other sex. Much of this early socialization transpires within the crucible of the family system.

Following the question raised in the chapter title, if the God figure is not posited as the chief motivating factor for moral behavior, is it accurate to say that there would be no basis for moral behavior? Certainly not. What is true is that children of both sexes will tend to base their moral beliefs on a God-based ethic *if* their parents and teachers socialize and educate them at an early age in this model and according to the correlates of such a theology. The preconventional morality of Kohlberg's stages 1 and 2 focuses almost exclusively on the themes of fear, punishment, obedience, and reward. These stages easily relate to a religious theme of sin and forgiveness. Often, although not always and not necessarily, these themes are, in fact, God-dependent. In Kohlberg's second level, conventional morality, stages 3 and 4 focus on social interaction and reciprocity as the motivators that serve to establish the norms of human behavior. As such, they are not God-dependent or theology-dependent.

---

[4] Gilligan points out that the psycho-social system of Erik Erikson is likewise deficient in that Erikson holds to the importance of passing through the *identity* stage prior to the *intimacy* stage of development. Gilligan claims that the female often seeks her identity via her attachment to a male, thus "Intimacy goes along with identity, as the female comes to know herself as she is known, through her relationships with others." Op. Cit. 12. Gilligan's work, along with that of Nancy Chodorow, stands as a much needed corrective to the tendency of developmentalists to equate human development with male development.

In short, research in child development, human development, and family development serves to establish the validity of the concept of stages of growth, even if the characterization of each stage remains somewhat controversial. Furthermore, the so-called God-hypothesis is neither a *necessary* nor a *sufficient* cause for the teaching of moral behavior. Reference to God is not necessary; legions of children are raised without reference to deity and yet develop their moral sense well into stages 4 and 5. Reference to God is not sufficient because even if there is reference to deity and religious tradition, other social forces tend to predominate that have little to do with substantiation of a God theme. Two of these social forces are the desire to be thought well of by ones' peers (social acceptance) and the strong force of social conformity.

Religion and Morality

Insofar as Christian theology is based on the Genesis story of Adam and Eve and the consequent punishment (Kohlberg stage 1) for disobedience, there can be little doubt that such theology is at the level of Kohlberg Stage 1. Christian theology is further based on the so-called theory of penal substitution, i.e., Jesus, by his death on the cross, took upon himself the punishment due us for our prime sin of disobedience as well as our alleged ordinary sins, thereby giving mortals the possibility of the reward of forgiveness, atonement, and reconciliation. This reward is Kohlberg stage 2. The Roman Catholic Church reenacts this drama through both the Mass and the confessional. Likewise, fundamentalist, evangelical, reformed, and even some liberal Christians hold to this theme of punishment and reward.

In contrast, nontheistic religions, especially Buddhism, readily pass beyond punishment and reward into Kohlberg's stages 3 and 4. The emphasis on selflessness, sacrifice, universal love, acceptance, and forgiveness often reach into Kohlberg's stage 5. Albert Schweitzer's emphasis on reverence for life, Mother Teresa's selfless life and ministry, Gandhi's peaceful resistance to British hegemony, and Martin Luther King Jr.'s leadership in peaceful civil disobedience are time-honored examples of morality that is not based on threat of punishment and promise of reward.

Kant's "Categorical Imperative"

A categorical imperative is a rational principle of ethical behavior that is unconditional and universally applicable.[5] The two primary formulations of Immanuel Kant's (1724–1804) categorical imperative state:

1. Act only on a maxim that you should wish to become a universal law.
2. Treat humanity, whether yourself or another, in every case as an end in itself, never as a means only.[6]

The first formulation is the principle of *universalization,* wherein the test of the rightness of an act is judged by whether one can, in good conscience, will that the contemplated action be universalized, i.e., practiced or willed by everyone. The second formulation is the principle of *means versus ends* in the treatment of fellow humans. The goal is to treat others as ends in themselves, not as means to the achievement of our own ends or purposes. According to W. T. Jones, these two formulations merge as "my duties to others would be no different from my duties to myself, and my rights would be identical with theirs."[7]

Kant's categorical imperative, in my opinion, encapsulates the essence of Kohlberg's postconventional stages 5 and 6. If stage 6 is out of sight for mortals, at least stage 5 is within our human range.

Eudaemonism as the Basis for a Human-Centered Ethic

What does a truly enlightened ethic of human moral behavior look like? *Eudaemonism* (Greek: *eu* [good] and *daemon* [demon—spirit being]) is usually translated as *well-being.*[8] Aristotle defined eudaemonism as the essence of happiness. Happiness is not to be understood as pleasure. Pleasure is a fleeting emotion. By its very nature it rises and falls, waxes and wanes. Happiness, in contrast to pleasure, is the state of living as closely as possible

---

[5] *Merriam-Webster's Collegiate Dictionary,* Eleventh Edition, 2003: A moral obligation or command that is unconditionally and universally binding.

[6] W. T. Jones, *A History of Western Philosophy* (New York: Harcourt, Brace, and Company, 1952) 852–858.

[7] Ibid. 856.

[8] *Merriam-Webster's Collegiate Dictionary,* Eleventh Edition, 2003: A theory that the highest ethical goal is happiness and personal well-being.

to the fulfillment of one's potentiality. As such, we may refer to it as self-fulfillment, self-realization, or self-actualization.[9]

In my view, Kant's categorical imperative is an integral part of an eudaemonistic ethic. Such an ethic seeks the well-being of all people. Well-being may be understood as including mental and physical health, living as close to fulfillment of one's potentiality as possible, and utilizing one's human talents and resources for the good of humankind. The quest for well-being plays out in the world of aesthetics, ethics, and politics. It is communitarian as well as individualistic; i.e., it has to do with human associations within the local community as well as the international community. The quest for the greatest good for the greatest number, including not just the choice of the greatest good, but also on occasion the choice of the lesser of evils, is congruent with an ethic of eudaemonism.[10] Within the business and industrial community, an ethic of well-being would extend to relationships between capital and labor, management and sales. Certainly such an ethic has strong implications for the stock market and such corporate entities as Enron, Worldcom, Wal-Mart, and Tyco.[11]

Following Kant's categorical imperative, I hold that eudaemonism is built upon the three additional imperatives of equality, responsibility, and honesty. Equality between races, classes, and ethnic backgrounds as well as between males and females is an absolute prerequisite for a meaningful sense of well-being.[12]

Responsibility for oneself and one's relationships in all endeavors, including the self in relationship to the seats of power in the community and society at large, is absolutely essential to a eudaemonistic ethic. While this responsibility begins with self-responsibility for one's own actions and existence, it extends to boards of corporations, town and city councils, and public boards of education. This responsibility extends both to internal matters and to the general public.[13]

---

[9] Aristotle, "Pleasure and Happiness," from *Nicomachean Ethics*.

[10] The utilitarianism of John Stuart Mill and Jeremy Bentham.

[11] See: Reinhold Niebuhr, *Moral Man and Immoral Society: A Study of Ethics and Politics* (New York: Charles Scribner's Sons, 1932). Also see: Harold H. Titus, *Ethics For Today* (Belmont, California: Wadsworth Publishing Company, Fifth Edition, 1973).

[12] Crosby, John F., *Sexual Autonomy: Toward a Humanistic Ethic*. (Springfield, Ill.: Charles C. Thomas, Publisher; 1981). Part II "Issues in Ethics," Chapters 7–12.

[13] Corporate responsibility applies to the stock market as well as to large corporate conglomerates such as Enron, Worldcom (MCI), and Tyco. For far too long, the religious communities have focused almost exclusively on individual ethics rather than on corporate ethics. It appears that theism and theistic religion has nothing to say to the corporate community and to the boards of directors and CEO's of corporate entities.

THE FLIPSIDE OF GODSPEAK

Honesty, in its most practical sense, implies being straightforward and acting in accordance with what we see as the best interests of people within our immediate community of life as well as the world around us. Honesty implies an ethic of truth based on both the correspondence theory of truth and the coherence theory of truth.

I submit to the reader that the blending of the three imperatives of equality, responsibility, and honesty with the two formulations of the categorical imperative (universality and means versus ends) constitutes an ethic of eudaemonistic quality. If the ethic is taken seriously and practiced equally among all people and in all situations, it will lead to a viable and pragmatic norm of human behavior and bring the bearer an inner sense of personal integrity and authenticity of selfhood.[14]

My conclusion to the question posed as the title to this chapter and the previous one, "Can there be morality without God?" is a resounding *yes*. On the positive side, there are countless legions of highly ethical and moral people who do not believe in God. On the negative side there appear to be countless believers who bear witness to the fact that belief in God makes little, if any, difference in the daily questions of personal morality as well as in the arena of public, corporate, and political life. Belief in God appears to be neither a prerequisite for moral behavior nor a necessary and/or sufficient condition for moral behavior.

Further, when inquiry is made concerning ethical issues such as abortion, birth control, euthanasia, stem cell research, gun control, global warming, and environmental pollution, belief in God appears to make little, if any, difference. In this sense, the implications of certain of humankind's values and beliefs become issues of great ethical and moral importance, not just to the present generation but to future generations. It would appear that the more the mind becomes set on a God-based code of morals, the more it becomes closed to the philosophical questioning so necessary in the study of human values and systems of ethical norms. Not only has God-based morality failed in terms of the socialization of children and youth, it has blatantly failed in terms of the failure of thorough and rigorous application on the part of adult leadership to the industrial, corporate, and government spheres of national life.

---

[14] For a more extensive treatment of eudaemonism see: Crosby, *Sexual Autonomy: Toward A Humanistic Ethic*, Part II, "Issues in Ethics," Chapters 7–12.

Teaching Children Morality

I conclude this chapter with my response to the question about what children can be taught about honesty and morality apart from an ethic based on punishment and reward. It is well established that early parental emphasis on altruistic and socially responsible behavior in a context of love and mutual support is both a necessary condition for and sufficient cause of responsibly moral behavior. An ethic of well-being based on the golden rule, Kant's categorical imperative, and the triple eudaemonistic principles of equality, responsibility, and honesty can be taught—and frequently is taught—to children of all ages and from all cultures and societies.[15] Once again we turn to Jean Piaget, who believed the "child's individual level of cognitive development, enhanced by informal interactions with other children, determines how the child characteristically thinks about right and wrong. Though Piaget's work was done many years ago, subsequent investigations have generally supported his findings."[16]

Suffice it to say that when parents fail to understand the child's emerging capacities for cognitive thought, and instead threaten the child with an ethic of corporal and divine punishment and the need for penitence and forgiveness for normal childhood and youth misbehaviors, the end result will not be a happy one. Such teaching and socialization will lead to internalization of a negative sense of self and will often result in a young adult laden with painful guilt and irrational shame.

Is morality without God possible? Absolutely. Is morality without God desirable? Absolutely. It is more desirable than at almost any time in human history because the God record is so terribly poor in its results. A eudaemonistic ethic based on ethical humanism, shorn of divine propaganda about the "proper" treatment of females and also shorn of the divine call for the destruction of peoples and cultures different from one's own, is much to be preferred to the superstitious and fear-based theologies created by humankind.

---

[15] Sandra Crosser, "Emerging Morality: How Children Think About Right and Wrong." Excelligence Learning Corporation, http://www.earlychildhood.com/Articles/index.cfm?.
[16] Ibid.

Chapter Eight

The Quest for Meaning and Purpose in Life

ACCORDING TO the answer to the first question of the *Westminster Shorter Catechism of Faith,* the "chief end of man is to glorify God, and enjoy Him forever." If for the Westminster divines the purpose of life is to glorify God and enjoy Him forever, then it is no stretch to say that the purpose and meaning of human existence is in the glorification and enjoyment of God.

As we discussed in Chapter Four, just as there are the traditional arguments for the existence of God based on the "uncaused first cause" (primal causality) and ontology (being), there is also the argument from design, referred to as *teleology. Theological* teleology (from Greek *telos*, end, goal, fulfillment, or purpose; and *logos*, theory, account, study) is the idea that God has a purpose in creation and that human creatures are part of a divine plan, a cosmological design that encompasses all creation. This in turn gives meaning and purpose to life in general and to individual lives in particular. *Philosophical* teleology may be defined as either "Nature itself is the result of an intention or purpose," or "Nature is the instrument by which a goal or result is achieved."[1]

If there is no God, then theological teleology is quite beside the point. Philosophical teleology, however, remains relevant for those who believe there is an *inherent* goal or purpose *within* nature. To argue that nature is the result of some greater purpose is to posit an intentionality behind, above, or beyond nature. This comes close to the belief that there is some power directing nature. To argue, on the other hand, that nature is an instrument by which a goal or result is achieved also implies an intentionality

---

[1] John Herman Randall Jr. and Justus Buchler, *Philosophy: An Introduction* (New York: Barnes & Noble, Inc. 1942) 162, 1965 paperback edition.

or purpose, but it does not necessarily imply any extraneous intention or purpose. The purpose can be inherent in nature itself.

Existentialism

An existential philosophical position will deny any extrinsic intentionality or purpose. In its most basic form, existentialism holds that existence precedes essence and not the other way around (i.e., essence precedes existence).[2] By definition, an essence or meaning that precedes existence is bound to be teleological in nature. Essence preceding existence implies a plan or a blueprint or some sort of intention that in some way guides the processes of the natural order. By this method of reasoning, a theist may believe that evolution is the means by which God achieves purpose within the created order. Historically, Christian theology has taught that human beings are given life in order to fulfill God's plan and purposes. A Christian, therefore, seeks to know and to understand the *will of God*. Liberal Christians often define this pre-given (a priori) meaning in a general manner, while more conservative Christians define meaning in a more specific and individualized manner.[3]

Existentialism holds that *existence precedes essence*. First is the fact of existence, and then comes the challenge to provide, define, or identify meaning. An existentialist will hold that only we ourselves can give meaning and purpose to our existence. In other words, meaning does not come from without, only from within. Some people claim to be Christian existentialists. This requires humans to be the meaning-givers and responsible for their own choices and decisions without any apriori meaning from the deity. Thus, a Christian existentialist may hold to belief in God but *not* in the idea that this God gives some sort of preordained and individualized meaning to a person's existence.

---

[2] *Webster's New World Dictionary*, Third College Edition (New York: Simon & Schuster, 1988). *Existentialism* is defined: "a philosophical and literary movement, variously religious and atheistic, stemming from Kierkegaard and represented by Sartre, Heidegger, etc.: it is based on the doctrine that concrete, individual existence takes precedence over abstract, conceptual essence and holds that human beings are free and responsible for their acts..." *Essence* is defined: "that which makes something what it is, intrinsic, fundamental nature or most important quality (of something); essential being." "The inward nature of anything, underlying its manifestations."

[3] Leslie D. Weatherhead, *The Will of God* (New York: Abingdon Press, 1944). This small treatise sets out the liberal Christian view of God's will being a generalized will that may be subdivided into intentional will, circumstantial will, and ultimate will.

A philosophical existentialist holds neither to a belief in deity as a supernatural power nor to there being any implied or pre-given meaning or purpose in one's existence. *Life is its own meaning.* This implies that humans are the meaning-makers or the meaning-givers. It is we who must struggle to define for ourselves the meaning and purpose, the goals and the objectives of our own limited time on planet earth.

Erich Fromm addresses the problem of meaninglessness and the inner restlessness that is associated with it. He states: "There is only one solution to his [humankind's] problem: to face the truth, to acknowledge his fundamental aloneness and solitude in a universe indifferent to his fate, to recognize that there is no power transcending him which can solve his problem for him. Man must accept the responsibility for himself and the fact that only by using his own powers can he give meaning to his life. . . . If he faces the truth without panic he will recognize that there is no meaning to life except the meaning man gives his life by the unfolding of his powers, by living productively."[4] For Fromm, living productively translates into the realization and actualization we have previously spoken about. It is not a productivity associated with the producing of things, but rather a productivity associated with an ongoing endeavor to live up to one's potential in the Aristotelian sense, i.e., to be the agent bringing about one's own fulfillment.

Value and Meaning

How do we become the "productive" personality that Fromm talks about? How do we identify, label, and define meaning and value for ourselves? The answer lies in what we value. Meaning, basically, is a derivative of what we value, of what we hold dear for ourselves, of what we treasure and experience to be of worth. Whenever we hold a montage of values that are congruent with each other (i.e., fit together without conflict into a harmonious whole), there issues forth a configuration of value. This configuration of value gives meaning and purpose to each individual value as well as to the whole, which becomes greater than the sum of the parts. "When values, however paradoxical they may be, form a configuration and when they are congruent with each other, life takes on its own meaning in the sense that the meaning of human existence is intrinsic to the very process of living. When values are congruent, they may be quite different and include a

---

[4] Erich Fromm, "Chapter Three, Human Nature and Character," in *Man For Himself.* (New York: Holt, Rinehart, and Winston, 1947)

wide range of possibilities, but they are not in conflict. They are compatible, i.e., they fit in with each other and form a configuration that consists of many parts. A true configuration of values allows for human diversity, spontaneity, and growth. Thus, the meaning that one chooses to give to one's existence is greater than the sum of the several parts because these parts interact, complement, and otherwise feed into each other, forming a holistic pattern."[5]

I cannot emphasize strongly enough that meaning in human existence is not a divine or supernatural mystery. It has nothing, per se, to do with traditional religion as understood in a Judeo-Christian sense or an Islamic sense. Simply stated, meaning is the byproduct of what we value. In this sense, if a person *genuinely* values his/her religion (not just superficially or nominally), this in itself can give meaning to that person's life, especially if this value is not in conflict with any other values. It is one thing to hold belief in God as a value that may add a measure of meaning and purpose to one's life. It is quite another thing to believe that it is God that injects meaning into human existence (traditional Judeo-Christian thought) much as a physician or nurse injects a fluid into one's arm by using a syringe.

The relationship between value and meaning is forthright (linear) and circular. This is to say that whatever we value is bound to bring us a sense of satisfaction, whether in the pursuit of it, the achievement of it, or the possession of it. To the extent that we value things, we may find meaning in pursuing them, achieving them, or possessing them. Sometimes the possession of things proves tedious and boring, and we look back and realize it was the effort expended to pursue and to achieve that made the thing or object meaningful. In this regard it is not difficult to find entrepreneurs and industrialists who, although of age, refuse to retire. The meaning of their existence is bound up with the making of money. This has value for them. They often already possess great wealth, yet they remain unsatisfied. For these people it is the pursuit and achievement that has value, not the possession. Their multiplicity of expensive possessions does not give meaning and satisfaction. Only in the making of money do they find satisfaction. Only in the game of endless accumulation do they find meaning and personal fulfillment.

The reader may protest that such pursuit is vainglorious and materialistic in the extreme. Nevertheless, to the extent the entrepreneur or CEO values the quest, there will be some measure of meaning for him or her. The philosophical study of values, *axiology,* often divides values into two

---

[5] John F. Crosby, *Illusion and Disillusion: The Self in Love and Marriage*, 4th ed. (Belmont, Calif.: Wadsworth Publishing Company, 1991) 198.

groups, moral values and aesthetic values. Truth, justice, honesty, integrity, etc., may be characterized as moral values. Aesthetic values may be characterized as related to beauty. Further, there is the ongoing issue of whether values are subjective or objective, that is, whether beauty is in the eye of the beholder or is inherent in the thing itself. Do values belong to objects and events, or do people endow things and events with value? If the value of a diamond is attributed to or ascribed by some authority, such as a jeweler, it will be placed on the retail market as having value based on its size and shape, its consistency and clarity. We call this its objective, or its intrinsic, value, that is, its value in itself, as a diamond. But if we ascribe value to a diamond, as in the case of an engagement ring, because of what it means to us, it takes on a different kind of value. It symbolizes our love for someone and our commitment to our relationship, which is subjective and extrinsic to the diamond itself. Intrinsic value comes from the thing itself. Extrinsic value comes from signification and representation, i.e., the significance and symbolic value of an object to the person who owns it.

Value is often generated by both objective and subjective factors, and the result is a compounding of both intrinsic value and extrinsic value. An example of such a double measure of value, i.e., the combination of both intrinsic and extrinsic value, is the value placed upon sexual relations by committed couples. First is the value in the act of interplay and intercourse. This value would be termed intrinsic to the pleasure associated with the entire sexual dance. An additional value is realized when the sexual dance is shared by two partners who are committed to each other in a total configuration of *agape* love, *philos* love, and *eros* love. This is the extrinsic value of sexual intimacy that points to the love bond as a symbolic value in its own right. (The most powerful argument for fidelity within marriage is that sexual relations can deliver two kinds of value and thus two different types of meaning: the pleasure, fun, and excitement of the sexual dance, as well as the ongoing satisfaction of two people similarly committed in their ongoing bond of love.)

The presence of both objective and subjective value and of intrinsic and extrinsic methods of valuation produces meaning in personal existence. Meaning is the result of what we value. More and greater ways of valuation give rise to greater and richer sources of meaning. Over the long haul, what we value little, we treasure lightly, simply because it does not have much meaning for us. So-called hollow victories illustrate this. When things come to us very easily, without toil and sacrifice, we sometimes cannot understand why they don't really mean much to us. On the other hand, that which is hard fought for and for which many sacrifices have been made

THE FLIPSIDE OF GODSPEAK

is usually highly valued and thus yields a greater depth of meaning and personal significance. Thomas Paine, the author of the famous little treatise published during the American revolution, *The Crisis*, wrote "The harder the conflict the more glorious the triumph. What we obtain too cheap, we esteem too lightly. 'Tis dearness only that gives everything its value."[6]

The degree to which we value something is an integral part of the equation. Rollo May says this succinctly: "The degree of an individual's inner strength and integrity will depend on how much he himself believes in the values he lives by."[7] In other words, if the values a person thinks he/she lives by are truly not his/her own, then they will not yield the meaning about which we are speaking. If the so-called values are merely pseudovalues or quasivalues—not really one's own but perhaps absorbed from parents and family—then they will not be productive of genuine meaning. An example of this is to be found in the religious tenets of countless people who simply no longer find any meaning in the religious symbols of their youth. They "sort of" believe in the God of their childhood and youth but no longer take seriously the affirmations of faith that were part of their baptism or confirmation. This indicates an erosion of faith resulting in their no longer believing as they once did. The result of breaking away from one's early teaching and belief oftentimes brings a sense of meaninglessness, emptiness, and despair with concomitant feelings of depression and dread. This is because they have lost the value and its ensuing meaning and have not yet learned how to replace the lost value with new values and new ways of being.

Another example of lost value is in the experience of those who have broken away from parental/societal patterns and traditional models of marriage and sex. Some of these folks have opted for a variety of partners in their adult lifestyle, claiming that marriage and the idea of life-long monogamy is an old-fashioned and outdated value. These folks claim to live their lives based on a new value of transient, interim partnerships. Many of those who genuinely believe in their new lifestyle will be successful in affirming new dimensions of meaning based on their new value system. Others will find little of lasting significance and meaning because they really do not believe in the values by which they are living.

Perhaps the greatest challenge in facing divorce and remarriage, the challenge of a blended family, is in the continuance of meaningful relations with children who may now be under the custody of a former wife or hus-

---

[6] Thomas Paine, *The Crisis*, Number I, December 23, 1776.
[7] Rollo May, *Man's Search for Himself* (New York W. W. Norton, 1953). Chapter 6, "The Creative Conscience"

band. While one configuration of value is broken via divorce, there is yet another configuration of value needing renewed commitment and constant nourishment.

Defining and Redefining One's Values

The crux of defining and giving meaning to one's life, this single experience of existence on planet Earth, depends entirely upon the values we choose to live by. Historically speaking, values were often thought of in abstract categories such as truth, goodness, justice, mercy, love, kindness, freedom, equality, and beauty. We hear a lot of talk about religious values and spiritual values. We also hear a lot about family values, especially slanted in a political or partisan manner. Of course we hear talk of moral values or the lack thereof.

Values must not be thought of exclusively in such abstract terms. In other words, value is both a noun and a verb. To value is to assign worth to, to rate in importance, to esteem highly. Does it bring personal satisfaction? Does it bring a sense of pleasure, a sense of pride, or a feeling of accomplishment? Does it represent a significant investment of oneself in some cause or some project? How much do we value our work or means of earning a living? How much do we value knowledge acquired through study and reading? How much do we value friendship? How much do we value creativity in the arts, in music, in crafts, in various hobbies and leisure-time pursuits? How much do we value our mate, our children, and our grandchildren? How much do we value our extended family and those of our kin who have preceded us?

How much do we value our country and its ideals? One of the most distressing signs of our time is the repeated appeal to values by politicians and political parties in the United States. This is nothing more than an appeal to baser instincts, as if the constituency of one party is above reproach, while the other party is somehow lost in a value vacuum or wasteland. We see the same phenomenon in various religious groups and denominations wherein one group waxes superior over the alleged shame and degradation of another.

Coping With the Loss of God

If God is a value to one and if faith in God is genuinely one's own, it will be an important factor in one's quest for meaning in life. On the other hand, if a person loses a faith that was once vital and dynamic, God and theism are no longer viable as ideals of value or worth.

For some people this loss creates a vast void, perhaps not greatly mourned at first, but a void nevertheless. Such a person will experience a loss of meaning in his/her personal existence unless or until the individual creates a new purpose and sense of meaning that will serve to fill the void.

This is my personal experience in my loss of faith that I relate in *Appendix I*. This is the loss that Paul Tillich describes so well in *The Courage To Be*.[8] And the stark fact is that no force can fill this emptiness and loss of meaning except the person himself/herself. Whenever we lose something of value—a friend, a vocation, a limb, our youth, our vitality—there will likely be a void that conveys a sense of meaninglessness, accompanied sometimes by despair, anxiety, and depression.

We may experience bereavement with the death of a mate or parent or, even more difficult, a son or daughter. Because there was love, there will inevitably be a terrible sense of loss. Can this loss be meaningful? Can this suffering provide a source of meaning? The answer is an unqualified yes. Suffering can be meaningful. Pain can be meaningful. Mental and emotional turmoil can be meaningful.

Perhaps no other writer of modern time has stated this as powerfully and eloquently as Viktor Frankl.[9] In telling of an encounter with a man who had lost his wife, Frankl challenges the man by pointing out that his depression at his wife's death is the inevitable result of the depth of the love that characterized the couple's dynamic marital relationship. "Suffering ceases to be suffering in some way at the moment it finds a meaning, such as the meaning of a sacrifice. . . . Man's main concern is not to gain pleasure or to avoid pain, but rather to see a meaning in his life."[10] This is Frankl's *will to meaning*, the essence of his *logotherapy*.[11]

Men and Women the Meaning Makers

The ultimate challenge of life is that of defining for ourselves a new center of existence, a new operational center of gravity, new foci and loci of value, purpose, and meaning. Tillich, commenting on Sartre's famous phrase "the

---

[8] Paul Tillich, *The Courage To Be* (New Haven: Yale University Press, 1952). See Chapter Two "Being, Nonbeing, and Anxiety."

[9] Viktor E. Frankl, *Man's Search For Meaning* (New York: Simon & Schuster, 1959).

[10] Ibid. (Paperback edition: Washington Square Press, Inc. 178–179).

[11] Ibid.

essence of man is his existence," says: "This sentence is like a flash of light that illuminates the whole Existentialist scene. One could call it the most despairing and the most courageous sentence in all Existentialist literature. What it says is that there is no existential nature of man, except in the one point that he can make of himself what he wants. Man creates what he is. Nothing is given to him to determine his creativity. The essence of his being—the 'should-be', 'the ought-to-be,'—is not something which he finds, he makes it. Man is what he makes of himself. And the courage to be as oneself is the courage to make of oneself what one wants to be."[12] This points to my own mantra regarding the meaning of human existence: *Life is its own meaning.*

The never-ending task of defining meaning for oneself and the ongoing challenge of discovering meaning in the myriad tasks of day-in and day-out living is no small accomplishment. In the simplest of terms, it means that there is no injection or infusion of meaning from outside ourselves. The existential challenge is to make sense of our one and only opportunity at life. Defining meaning and purpose for ourselves and endowing our life with value in all its various hues, shades, and levels amidst the vicissitudes of daily life becomes the very essence or meaning of life. In truth, there is no task or challenge more rewarding, because, finally, it is not how others value what you do or do not do with this singular existence, but how you value your own being, how you place worth on what you do with the gift of life. What we value not only says a lot about who we are, but also determines the very essence or meaning of our life.

Coda

In Appendix I, the reader will encounter the account of my loss of the Christian faith that I had enthusiastically embraced for many years. I relate the journey that led to my renunciation of my Presbyterian ordination vows. Now, after years of search and study in which I continually gave birth to myself, I realize that my denial of the traditional God of Christian, Islamic, and Judaistic theism continues to give me a great sense of relief! I am relieved of having to explain (primarily to myself) how such a loving God allows and permits human suffering. I am relieved of having to defend such an absent, silent, and distant god. I am relieved of having to explain the Holocaust. I am relieved of having to explain the Crusades of the Middle Ages and the burning of Servetus at the stake with John Calvin's consent. I

---

[12] Ibid., Chapter Three

THE FLIPSIDE OF GODSPEAK

am relieved of having to explain hurricanes, tornadoes, floods, earthquakes, fires, and volcanic eruptions. (Excluding that part caused by human folly, i.e., the over-building of dams and the overlay of concrete jungles causing floods, the destruction and laying waste of rain forests and the raping of the earth to obtain fossil fuels and then abandoning it without restoration.) Without the God of Christian, Islamic, and Judaistic theism, I am relieved of having to explain anomalies of nature such as Down's syndrome, spinal bifida, cancer of all types and descriptions, schizophrenia, and bipolar syndromes. I am relieved of having to explain a Hitler or a Stalin or any other ruthless dictator. I am also relieved of having to explain nationalistic leaders, generals, presidents, and demagogues who presume to aggress and destroy and kill in the name of their own personal God of love.

In other words, without the presence of such a theological godhead, life makes a lot more sense to me. With my former belief in the God of traditional theism, I had question after question as to why a loving father would permit the evil present in the world throughout history. Without this God, I now have far fewer questions. My expectations are lowered dramatically. I have no expectations associated with the concept of a loving father or a caring parent. I can face down the ravages of nature knowing full well the possibilities for horrendous destruction. I accept the world and life as a given without any reference to a supernatural 'giver.' I face life strictly on its own terms and without appeal to any supernatural force or author.

I concur with Richard Dawkins when he says: "All appearances to the contrary, the only watchmaker in nature is the blind forces of physics.... Natural selection, the blind, unconscious, automatic process which Darwin discovered, and which we now know is the explanation for the existence and apparently purposeful form of all life, has no purpose in mind... it has no mind and no mind's eye. It does not plan for the future. It has no vision, no foresight, no sight at all. If it can be said to play the role of watchmaker in nature, it is the *blind* watchmaker."[13]

The constructivism that I learned from Jean Piaget, Paul Watzlawick, and Ernst von Glasersfeld lets me embrace my own role as a creator and builder of meaning and purpose. Von Glasersfeld, in his concluding homage to Jean Piaget, spoke not simply of knowledge, but rather of the *generation* of knowledge, i.e., "the constructivist principle that we ourselves build our picture of the world in which we live."[14]

---

[13] Richard Dawkins, *The Blind Watchmaker* (New York: W.W. Norton & Company, 1986).

[14] Ernst von Glasersfeld, "Homage to Jean Piaget (1896–1980)," *Irish Journal of Psychology* 18(3), (1997) 293–306.

Afterword

Constructivist philosophy is the end of God talk and its often arrogant assumptions that exude piety and a presumptuous attitude. The Flipside of Godspeak marks the end of theism and theistic attempts to put an anthropomorphic face on the unknown. The Flipside of Godspeak is humility in the face of a vast and indifferent universe—yet a universe filled with the wonders of nature and of life's myriad mysteries. In the wake of constructivist thought, there is a sense of awe and wonder, a sense of beauty and splendor, a sense of honest angst rather than a sham security based on a mythical belief.

Four general trends characterize the belief patterns of those who embrace, in one form or another, the philosophy of constructivism. These four trends may blend together in varying proportions, especially trends two and three.

Trend one follows the lead of natural theology, wherein all the forces of the evolutionary process are respected and honored, but the concept of God is affixed to the process, so that the result is a modern day manifestation of deism. The idea of God becomes the philosophical "first cause" that is placed at the top of the pyramid as the absentee author or omnipotent force behind all creation.

Trend two is the movement toward a neospiritualism that seeks to help the individual enmesh himself/herself in an ambience of spirit-filled presence. It is an attempt to get beyond theism by relating oneself to nature and to the ages. Many people find this nontheistic spirituality to be dynamic and meaningful. For them, the Flipside of Godspeak is a spirit-filled journey wherein meaning is ascribed to the relation of the individual to the universe, a celebration of the tie that binds humankind to all of life.[1] This trend is somewhat in the tradition of Erich Fromm and John Dewey.

Trend three follows the Paul Tillich/John Spong emphasis on the God above the God of theism. The emphasis is on the absolute impossibility of

---

[1] One definition of religion emphasizes the root word, *ligare,* to bind, to bind together, to tie, i.e., in what manner is an individual tied or related to the universe?

defining the ultimate reality or supreme life force. Nevertheless, life is addressed as an expression or manifestation of this ultimate ground of being, even if it remains forever nameless.

Trend four is the total constructivist approach to theism, developed in Chapters One and Two, which claims the impossibility of direct knowledge of any ultimate force or ultimate reality. This mode of belief, existential and humanistic, goes beyond theism in that there is no reference to any transcendent or immanent reality or any necessary endorsement of spirit or spirituality. For many holding this view, life is a pilgrimage into continuing exploration, be it in the wonder of the cosmos or the microcosm of cellular creation. For others, the pilgrimage will be a journey bringing hope and some measure of succor and sustenance into the ghettos of human oppression and deprivation. People with this bent of mind will almost always focus their attention and energy on the human condition within both the natural order and the political order. The constructivist is always aware of the limitations of his/her mind and maintains an awe-filled humility in the face of the mysteries of the universe and the profound grandeur of life.

In each of the four trends, the constructivist approach rules out ill-considered and thoughtless claims about the will of a theistic deity. Constructivism puts in their place the logic of the evolutionary process and the continuing quest of humanity for a world free of homicidal warfare, needless disease, malnutrition, and starvation. Constructivism leads to world leadership acting not in the name of a holy jihad, but in the name and for the benefit of all peoples sharing planet Earth. Constructivism gives us a new language filled with moral honesty and integrity. It is a language that permits humankind to take both solace and strength in what Bishop John Spong refers to as the postmodern era.

> Yes, it is frightening to think that there is no heavenly parent in the sky who will take care of us. We recall that moment in our human maturing process when we realized that we had become adults and that we, therefore, had to be responsible for ourselves. No earthly parents could protect us any longer. Perhaps we cushioned that experience with the theistic God premise. . . . The realization is dawning that we human beings are alone and therefore are responsible for ourselves, that there is no appeal to a higher power for protection. We are learning that meaning is not external to life but must be discovered in our own depths and imposed on life by an act of our own will."[2]

---

[2] John Shelby Spong, *Why Christianity Must Change Or Die* (San Francisco: Harper SanFrancisco, 1998) 69.

Afterword

Hopefully, for all of us, the end result of a constructivist philosophy will be a celebration of life bespeaking a deep gratitude and humility under the umbra of life itself, wherein truth, honesty, equality, and total responsibility for oneself form the basis of an ethic of well-being for all humankind.

Appendix I

Confession of an Apostate

IN THE beginning, my life was dedicated to God. My parents saw to that. No, they did not push and prod. They simply had me baptized and saw to it that the church was the center of both my religious life and my social life. Everything that came after was essentially my own doing. I took the church and its confessional *kerygma* (Jesus is Lord) seriously. I took it into myself. I internalized the teachings of Jesus. I internalized the orthodox Christian teaching about the trinity.

Then, fast forwarding to 1970, after having resigned my last pulpit in 1967, I was scheduled to appear before the Presbytery of Cayuga-Syracuse for my formal *demitting*, the Presbyterian terminology for leaving the ministry, more commonly known as *defrocking*. I had given a five-minute encapsulated version of my reasons for wanting to leave the ministry. After the unanimous vote for dissolution by the Presbytery, I walked alone down the long center aisle to the exit. I kept my eyes glued to the floor, not wanting to make eye contact with anyone. "You could hear a pin drop on the carpet," my friend and fellow cleric said to me in the vestibule. To those watching, I must have looked solitary and forlorn, but in truth I had just relieved myself of a tremendous burden. I was happy. I was free at last. I had just renounced my ordination vows. I was no longer under Holy Orders, as some would later say. I was no longer an ordained minister of the United Presbyterian Church in the U.S.A.

At my ordination in 1956, 14 years before, after finishing my ministerial education at Princeton Theological Seminary, I had received the laying on of hands. In those intervening years, I did the work of a pastor in three different churches. I performed weddings, officiated at funerals, visited the sick, founded a church, and handled the details of church administration. But in the 10th year something went terribly wrong. God and I had a fall-

Appendix I

ing out. One of us had to back off. One of us had to retreat. One of us had to die. And it was not going to be me.

In truth, my metamorphosis was a long time in the making. I had always been a doubter of the first rank. As a philosophy major at Denison University, I simply could not accept many of the easy answers of Christian orthodoxy. Even at Princeton Seminary, I could not swallow the conservative line of many of my classmates. I certainly never believed in the physical resurrection of Jesus. Perhaps it was simply the power of belief of those who claim to have seen the risen Christ. I had no trouble accepting the fact that no one really knows the birth date of Jesus. I never believed in the so-called virgin birth, the belief that the Holy Spirit provided the 23 male chromosomes that would match with Mary's 23 female chromosomes. The Roman Catholic belief that Mary's mother conceived Mary immaculately (untainted by coitus with a male) I found amusing, if not laughable.

I had no trouble accepting most of the findings of rigorous Biblical scholarship and the disciplines of the lower (textual) and higher (historical) criticisms.[1] In the Old Testament, this included the weaving together of various documents of the Pentateuch by editors known as redactors. This became known as the *documentary* theory, the Graf-Wellhausen theory, that is the four strands of the Pentateuch that came to be known as JEDP. (J=Jehovah/Yahweh; E=Elohim; D=Deuteronomic; and P=Priestly). I had no difficulty with the fact of there being two Genesis stories of creation, the one being the seven-day creation myth (Genesis 1:1-2:3, from the P or Priestly strain) and the other the Garden of Eden account (Genesis 2:4-4:26, the J [Y] or Jehovah/Yahweh strain). Of course I was never one to take either of these stories literally.

I had no trouble with the theoretical foundation of the four Gospels as arising from material that came from the hypothesized source known as Q (Quelle=Source) combining with Mark's original material. Matthew and Luke then built on both Mark and Q with their own private sources, M and L. (*The Gospel of Thomas*, 114 sayings of Jesus, dating to late first century CE, was discovered in 1945 near the town of Nag Hammadi in Upper Egypt and was apparently unknown to my seminary professors in those days. Or, if it was ever mentioned, it passed me by without a blink.)

I always had trouble with the miracle stories. In my years in the pulpit, I usually tried to explain them away with some attempt at a rational

---

[1] Lower or textual criticism is the study of the text using the tools of exegesis and linguistics, including grammar, style, phraseology, and etymology. Higher criticism, or historical criticism, is the attempt to answer questions such as who wrote the passage, when, for what purpose, and for whom.

explanation. An example of this was the feeding of the 5,000. (Matthew 14:13–21). A somewhat logical explanation would be the fact that once Jesus and the disciples began to share their two fish and five loaves, the crowds took this as a sign that they could now dig into their own bread baskets and begin eating their own fish and loaves. Many ministers simply spiritualize the story, saying that when we share what we have, there is sufficient food for all. In point of fact, I suspect most ministers of the more liberal Christian denominations spiritualize the resurrection in the same manner, saying that what really happened is that the risen Christ came into the hearts and minds of believers. A careful reading of the resurrection accounts shows that only those who first believed in the risen Lord were enabled to actually see him. (Remember Thomas, who insisted on seeing the risen Lord before he would believe: John 20:24–29. Paul's conversion experience on the Road to Damascus is not considered one of the Gospel resurrection accounts.) The main distinction between the reality of the earthly/human Jesus and the dogma of the living Christ of faith lies in whether or not a person believes that Jesus is present in an enduring, personal, and spiritual sense.

 I also had great difficulty with *eschatology*, the doctrine of the last times, and apocalyptic literature. I found the Revelation of John, the last book in the New Testament, not worth bothering with. I do not think I preached a single sermon in 11 years based on John's nightmarish vision. Saint Paul, who complained about a thorn in his flesh (II Corinthians 12:7), was always a thorn to me. Paul seemed to theologize everything and built his entire message on his encounter with the allegedly risen Christ. It is Paul who constructs and reconstructs the penal-substitutionary theory of the atonement, the theory most popular among conservative and fundamentalist Christians today. It was popular from the earliest times of the Roman and Greek Orthodox churches, and then it became the staple belief of St. Augustine and later Martin Luther and John Calvin at the time of the Protestant Reformation. This theory builds on the alleged sin of Adam, who disobeyed God in the Garden of Eden. Disobedience becomes the pivotal foundation upon which the need for forgiveness and salvation is built. By enduring crucifixion, Jesus took upon himself the punishment due each one of us because of Adam's disobedience in taking a bite from the fruit offered him by Eve. This story also lays the foundation for 4,000 years of prejudice and discrimination against the female sex.[2] The whole idea of

---

[2] It is worthy of note that Paul is largely responsible for the very low view of marriage that became popular from the second century onward in the Common Era. "It is ironic that the Christians should have drastically lowered the status of marriage. Yet, under Christian

divine punishment for sin was as repugnant to me in my years as a minister as it is today. Whenever I hear that Jesus died for me, I immediately think of World War II and places like Pearl Harbor, Midway, and Normandy, when thousands upon thousands of young men stormed the beaches on D day. Thousands of them died for me.

In all of this, my quarrel was never really with Jesus, nor with my role as minister, pastor, teacher, and preacher. My quarrel went right to the heart of the matter, i.e., God. In 1964, I slowly began to question everything. I became fascinated with the spate of books dealing with the so-called death of God. I read and reread bits and pieces of the great philosophers. Even St. Thomas's adaptation of Aristotle couldn't persuade me. I thought St. Augustine very arrogant. I never did think much of John Calvin. While I believed Martin Luther had excellent reason for breaking from the Holy See at Rome, I could not credit his theology as being either fresh or revolutionary. I became intrigued with the writings of Dietrich Bohnhoeffer, but I became disenchanted when I realized that he, much like Calvin and Luther, refused to deal with the question behind all questions: whether or not there exists such a being as God.

In 1965, as I felt my faith weakening and withering away, I turned to the writings of Kierkegaard, Nietzsche, Sartre, Kafka, and Camus. When I felt myself estranged from God, I turned in desperation to Leslie Weatherhead and Harry Emerson Fosdick, two of the most formidable liberal Protestant theologian-preachers of the first half of the twentieth century. After concluding that the question of God is 100 percent a matter of faith in an unknowable force, I parted with what is known as *revealed* theology.

Revealed theology is often contrasted with *natural* theology. Natural theology is based on the argument from design. We marvel at the natural order, the birthing of human infants and the cycles of nature, the wonders of the macro universe of stars and galaxies, the constant operation of the solar system. We ponder the wonders of the universe of plants, trees, flowers, rivers, waterfalls, the awful beauty of storms, and even catastrophic events such as floods, earthquakes, tornadoes, and hurricanes. In all of this, we reason from the fact of the created order to a force or object or being capable of creating such magnificent wonders. This was one of the chief

---

influence, marriage and the family were more lowly regarded than ever before, or since. . . . They became victims of a conception of marriage as a purely sexual union—as a slightly more desirable alternative than fornication." Gerald Leslie, *The Family In Social Context*, 5th ed. (New York: Oxford University Press, 1982) 175.

arguments used by St. Thomas Aquinas in his (alleged) proofs of the existence of God.

Revealed theology, on the other hand, claims that the only way humankind can know the reality and presence of an almighty God-Being is if this being chooses to reveal itself in a definite and purposeful way. To reveal is to "pull back the curtain," as in the theater, and to make known what was previously hidden from sight. Revealed Christian theology claims that the Jesus Christ event is God's way of revealing himself to humankind. Karl Barth, a Swiss Protestant theologian writing between the two world wars, is considered by many to be the most influential Christian theologian to proclaim the Jesus event as being the one essential pivotal instance of God making himself known to humans. Barth was a disillusioned liberal who claimed that liberal theology with its emphasis on the so-called "social gospel" was weak and misguided. Barth, in his commentary on the Book of Romans (*The Epistle to the Romans,* 1919) disdained the evidence of natural theology and claimed the Christ event to be the decisive intervention of God in the affairs of humankind. Barth's writings became the bedrock of what came to be called neoorthodoxy or crisis theology, which replaced the liberalism of men like Weatherhead and Fosdick.[3] This did not happen overnight, but it did encompass the twenties, thirties, forties, and fifties of the twentieth century.[4]

Looking back, I think it was neoorthodoxy, with its emphasis on revealed theology, that did me in. For a while I bought into it, especially when I was soaking up all I could from my professors at Princeton Seminary. My professors in theology were very high on the writings of Emile Brunner, a follower/disciple of Karl Barth. This was my terrible mistake. I suspended my own faculty of critical thought and bought into something I thought was wonderful and marvelous. To say I now regret this is a gross understatement.

---

[3] "The principal emphasis in Barth's work, known as neo-orthodoxy and crisis theology, is on the sinfulness of humanity, God's absolute transcendence, and the human inability to know God except through revelation. His objective was to lead theology away from the influence of modern religious philosophy, with its emphasis on feeling and humanism, and back to the principles of the Reformation and the prophetic teachings of the Bible. . . . For Barth, God's sole revelation of himself is in Jesus Christ." *Encarta,* s.v. Karl Barth.

[4] Barth was teaching in Bonn, Germany, in 1934 when Hitler suspended him from his academic position. Barth was key author of the *Barmen Declaration of 1934* that opposed the Nazi regime. He was deported to his native Switzerland in 1935. He came to the United States only once. That visit was to Princeton, where he gave a memorable lecture at the Princeton University Chapel in 1962. Barth died in 1968.

Appendix I

And then I crashed. It was a long slow crash, but it had a definite thud at the end. In my sermons all through 1965 and 1966, I had been struggling with the most basic of all theological concepts, the concept of God. I was extremely disappointed with the lack of discussion and consideration of the first person of the trinity in the new confession of faith that was passed by the Presbyterians in 1967, known as the *Confession of 1967*.

My prime stumbling block was the apparent (to me) absence of God in the affairs of the world. I saw no presence of God in the Vietnam fiasco. I saw no sign of God in the face of evil, or in the catastrophic events that seemed to me to overwhelm several of my parishioners. I had encountered the tragic and needless death of a child, a likewise tragic and needless death of a teenager, and a tragic and needless death of a young mother. These three deaths came within a very short span of time. Had they come years earlier and been spread out over a longer period of time, I probably could have accepted them as tragic and unfortunate events that come upon humankind, even upon persons whom you consider to be the crème de la creme and morally upright on earth. I could not believe these three deaths to be God's will or to have anything at all to do with God.[5] These three deaths led me further and further from the teachings of the church and of the Bible. I doubted if God was really a God of love. I doubted the promises of God about his being with us. I doubted everything I had ever learned and held dear about God. At age 34, I was a very angry young man. I saw no reason for God's distance and remoteness. I was sick and tired of explaining to people that God always answers prayer but that a lot of the time we do not pick up on these answers or the answers are not what we had hoped for.

In late 1965 I began to "tear." I did not cry tears. I simply developed the feeling of a tear always being present in one eye. The symptom haunted me. The most obvious interpretation was that I was grieving. What was I grieving? I had my eyes checked. I also took on the symptoms of night sweats. I would awaken in a cold/hot sweat for no apparent reason. I had a complete medical checkup. I was in prime physical health.

The "crash" came one day just as I completed the committal service of a fine gentleman.[6] His death was not tragic. It was a release. He was a man of years, and he had suffered enough. I remember giving the final benediction. I intoned the words I had used for almost 11 years: "…in the sure and certain hope of eternal life through our Lord Jesus Christ. Amen."

---

[5] These were the death of a young boy after heart surgery due to a mistake made by a surgical attendant; the death of a young wife and mother who took her own life; and the death of a teenage boy who perished in a violent snow storm.

[6] November 18, 1966.

As I walked away from the grave, it hit me like a thunderbolt. It was not a voice from outside me. Nor was it a voice talking to me from the inside. It was *me* talking to *me*. It was the "doubting" me speaking emphatically to the "believing" me. It was strong self-talk. The words came tumbling through my mind: "S—t! I don't believe a word of it."

At that instant my ministry was over. I knew that God and I were through with each other. Somehow the tremendous amount of energy necessary to keep my Christian belief system alive had simply become exhausted. It wasn't burnout from too much work. I did church administration well, and I loved preaching. It was a burnout of faith. At that moment, the truth simply burst in upon me, the truth that I no longer believed in God the father. Or in any god. Jesus still meant something to me. I wasn't sure just what. But I knew that I certainly didn't belong in a Presbyterian pulpit.

I think what happened was that my defenses, my psychological defense mechanisms and safety devices, finally caved in. I had been so well defended for so many years that it took a lot of repeated assaults to finally penetrate my defenses. I now believe that faith is based primarily on psycho-emotional need. This need is not necessarily present when we are young or when we first learn the faith. As we grow and mature, we internalize this belief, and the greater the degree of internalization, the more our entire sense of being and identity is engulfed in the belief. Then in later years, to think of parting with such a belief system becomes anxiety-producing in the extreme. It is as if one's entire underpinnings and infrastructure are threatened. I imploded with a battery of questions. Who am I? What am I? What is the meaning of human existence? What is the meaning of *my* existence? Of *my* life? Where shall I go? What shall I do? What about my three sons, aged seven, six, and three? My wife? What would my parents say?

I continued to walk away from the grave. I knew that I would be resigning my job as minister. Within 10 minutes, many scenarios passed through my mind. I went directly home and shared with Marjorie, my wife, what I had experienced. She knew that I had been wrestling with these issues, but I must admit that I didn't let her in fully on my struggles. In retrospect I think I had been protecting her. More likely I was really protecting myself! She seemed not to be surprised. Perhaps she had seen more of me than I had allowed myself to see. That night, as I spoke on the phone with Marjorie's father, I began to cry. The tears flowed. I hit my emotional low. I never cried again. The tearing continued for awhile, but as I allowed myself to grieve my loss, the tearing grew progressively less. I had lost my identity, my means of earning a livelihood, my immediate job, my career, and for a time my parents. Likewise, I had no more night sweats. The attacks of acute anxiety were in spontaneous remission.

I made a quick trip to New Jersey to consult with my father-in-law. He was a calming influence, communicating to me that he understood what I was experiencing. He was a liberal Presbyterian minister for whom I had worked in my student days. During this visit, I came upon a plan. I did not wish to lay a burden on the members of my church. This wasn't their struggle or their problem. I would make my exit gracefully and without fanfare or fuss of any kind. No parting shots or ill-advised sermons. My reason for leaving? I wanted to go back to school. Do a doctorate. But study what? Perhaps go into teaching. Living in the greater Syracuse area gave me wonderful access to a great university. It became my haven.

My congregation didn't need to know the details. I told them I was restless and was eager to pursue a new direction in my life. The important thing was to get out gracefully and not to cause them distress. Fortunately, when I first came to that church in 1962, I had asked for a rental allowance as part of my salary instead of living in the church manse. Neither my wife nor I liked the idea of manse living. We bought a modest ranch home. It was very comfortable and more than sufficient for three years of graduate school. All I had to do now was figure out how I could earn enough money to pay the monthly mortgage and other living expenses as well as tuition and books.

Being a traditionalist at that time, I had for years preferred that Marjorie not be gainfully employed. I discarded that idea in a hurry. She had a B.S. degree and an R.N. from Cornell University New York Hospital. So in August of 1967, she went to work and I became a full-time graduate student and a house husband.

I did my graduate work in the field of marriage and family relations under Professor Robert Pickett of Syracuse University. I did a minor in child development under Professor Betty Caldwell and another minor in clinical psychology. I also did my clinical training for eventual membership in the American Association for Marriage and Family Therapy (AAMFT), training under Harvey Nordsey.

The United Presbyterian Church had a policy of a one-year waiting period before an ordained minister could demit the ministry. I allowed myself three full years. In that period, I met with a committee of Presbytery on several occasions. Then in May of 1970, I went before Presbytery. It wasn't planned that I speak. I had told the committee of Presbytery that I preferred not to speak, but that if I did speak I wanted at least 15 minutes. When the motion came up for my demitting the ministry, a friend stood up and said he would not vote on the issue until he heard my reasons. The moderator pounded the gavel and said I could speak for no more than five minutes. What was I to say in five minutes?

I said simply that the older I got, the less I knew about God, his alleged existence, omnipotence, omniscience, and omnipresence. The most I could say was that I still admired the writings of Paul Tillich and that I cautiously identified, to a point, with Tillich's concept of "God above the god of theism."[7] I told the Presbytery that I wanted to be relieved of my ordination vows and that I no longer belonged in a Christian pulpit.

I cannot say that I followed the injunction of Jesus about never looking back.[8] I have looked back many times, but I have always come to the same conclusion. As the church and theology have become increasingly conservative, with a marked leaning to the far right and even to embracing simplistic and rigid fundamentalism, I have never doubted the wisdom that led me to do demit the ministry.

But the price was high. I have already spoken of the emotional price. There was also an energy price. There was what I call a family price and social price in the loss of friends. Through it, all there was a severe financial price. I begin with the financial, because it was throughout a source of great stress.

After struggling through the three years of graduate work with a fellowship, teaching assistantships, and a grant from the Joseph P. Kennedy Jr. Foundation,[9] I needed money to help me move my family to Bloomington, Indiana. I had accepted a teaching position at Indiana University. I tapped into my pension from the church. In the Presbyterian Church at that time, the minister paid three percent of his/her annual salary into the pension fund, and the church, as part of the minister's remuneration, paid an additional 10 percent. Because I had demitted the ministry, I was entitled only to the return of my accumulated three percent plus interest. The remaining 10 percent was not considered to belong to me, and so I was forever unable to retrieve it.[10]

---

[7] Paul Tillich, *The Courage To Be* (New Haven: Yale University Press, 1952)

[8] Luke 9:62. "No one who puts his hand to the plow and looks back is fit for the kingdom of God."

[9] Professor Betty Caldwell helped me immensely by steering me through the process of securing a grant with the Kennedy Foundation. I will always be appreciative of the positive backing of Eunice Shriver, who believed in and supported me in the creation of a family life and sex education curriculum for middle school/junior high students. I later taught and tested this curriculum in three different types of schools: a boys' military school, a country school district, and an inner-city school.

[10] When I turned 65, I attempted to retrieve the 10 percent plus interest. The authorities at

Appendix I

My paltry three percent tided us over and got us to Bloomington, Indiana, and the beginning of a new life. Yet there were wounds to be healed. When I explained to my parents, in the spring of 1970, that I was going before Presbytery to demit the ministry, my mother lashed out at me. In a bellowing outcry of emotion, very uncharacteristic of her, she screamed, "Oh, John, can't you wait until we're dead?"

I replied in a calm voice that it seemed to me that if she really cared about my happiness, she would rejoice with me that I had embarked on a new life and that I felt good about myself. Of course this did not sit well. Neither of my parents ever sat down with me to discuss the situation in a rational manner. As I was struggling in late 1965 and early 1966, I had tried to engage them in meaningful dialogue about my motivation for leaving the ministry. I wanted to share my thoughts, my conflicts, and my pain with them. I wanted to share my feelings of alienation and estrangement. I wanted to tell them about my doubts regarding the existence of God and the extent of God's alleged involvement in the everyday lives of people. This openness led to one short interchange in which I genuinely felt I had been heard, at least by my father. I remember thanking them for listening to me. Nothing of any depth was ever spoken between us again. We never again spoke about my leaving the ministry. I hold the assumption that both of my parents were ashamed to tell their friends. I learned in later years they had told few people, if any, of my crisis of faith and my self-imposed defrocking.

They told their friends, including their minister, that I had simply gone into teaching marriage and family studies and into family counseling. My dad and mother visited me once in Bloomington, and my father seemed genuinely pleased and interested in what I was doing. He died shortly after that, and I regret to this day that I didn't have more time to rebuild our relationship. I remember visiting their home on several occasions in 1971 and 1972 as dad's cancer progressed.

My mother and I did better after an interlude of estrangement. I think she finally realized that if we were to have a relationship, it would have to be built on my redefinition of myself as a professor, not as a minister. The most she ever said was, "We have so little in common to talk about." While she outlived my father by 14 years, our relationship never really became

---

the Presbyterian pension fund reminded me I had signed off on the 10 percent. Of course I had signed off, albeit under duress, because that was the only way I could retrieve my original three percent. I wanted to initiate a law suit but was advised, since these were pre ERISA days, that I would probably lose, and that if I won, it would likely cost more than I would gain.

vital or dynamic in any way. "Perfunctory" became the order of the day. My younger brother, an artist and professor, was not at all affected by my decision. To my knowledge, he never was a believer. We have enjoyed a fine relationship ever since. My sister remains a devout Christian. We have never discussed my leaving the ministry and the church, at least not in any depth. She seems quite happy and contented.

I do feel, however, that my family really did not want to openly discuss or deal with the fact that I had referred myself to psychotherapy. Early on in my struggle in January of 1966, I had entered into a therapeutic relationship with a highly regarded therapist who taught at the Upstate Medical Center in Syracuse. My therapist was very helpful to me as I struggled to redefine myself. I remember telling him that I wanted to find out *why* I went into the ministry in the first place. I wanted to explore what held me together all these years and what effect the ego rewards (certainly not financial) had upon me. My own take on this year of therapy remains to this day that it was a time of slowly unlearning my dependency upon God (to this point unseen and therefore unlabeled). I learned to give up my defenses and my entire psycho-emotional identity as a servant of God. This unlearning and externalizing came only as I internalized a new and strong belief in myself, learning to accept myself, trust myself, respect myself, and love myself. This was new to me. It changed my life. In truth, the year of psychotherapy helped me give birth to myself.

I have often wished I could have sat down in a room with my parents and a family-trained therapist and worked this whole thing through. I wish also that I had later involved my wife and my children in therapy with a family therapist. After all, the family system is such that the actions/ behavior of one member has a strong and powerful effect, even if hidden and muted, upon all other members of that family. Not only had I asked my mate to abandon her role as a traditional mother and housewife, I had asked her to earn half of our total living expenses. Again, this worked out well because Marjorie seemed to welcome a return to the nursing profession and, later, to nurse midwifery.

However, I'm afraid I didn't pay enough attention to the needs and transitional challenges facing my sons. My youngest became a nursery school dropout, hiding under a bed when it was time to go to school. He preferred to stay home with me and pretend to study with me. At times I felt my two older boys were relieved not to be called PKs (preacher's kids) any more. I distinctly remember coming to the belief that as important as my family was to me, the best thing I could do to reestablish myself as a breadwinner was to work diligently at my studies. I embraced the belief,

Appendix I

almost a mantra, that "If there were no *me*, there would be no *us*" (if I did not get my act together, we would not have a future as a family). With this thought powerfully etched in my mind, I resolutely set my life energy upon my doctoral program.

Last but by no means least, there was a social price. To be blunt, we lost friends. People who had befriended us now shunned us. Again, this revealed my naïve belief that people liked my wife and me because of *us*, not because of our role in the church and community. But former close friends simply ignored us. Perhaps they were threatened by my change in belief. Perhaps not. All I remember is that there was some degree of pain in all of this.

As much as I have enjoyed my teaching career at both Indiana University and the University of Kentucky, I would be less than candid if I did not admit that I still feel a tinge of a sense of loss. I lost God and all that the belief and commitment implied. I lost a livelihood that I basically liked. I liked the challenge of preaching on timely subjects and the challenge of creating and crafting weekly sermons (In those days, 48 sermons a year plus special occasions). The church I had founded and the other two that I served were, at the time, liberal, community-minded institutions.[11] They were socially relevant in the sense of being sensitive to community, national, and world issues.

I continue to study both the words of Jesus and the acts of Jesus as these have been included in the so-called quest of the historical Jesus.[12] This quest, first begun by David Friedrich Strauss, later made well known by Albert Schweitzer, and reaching recent expression via the discipline and writings of the Jesus Seminar, is one of the few legacies of the Christian faith to which I am able to relate in any meaningful manner.[13] In addition, I find the writings of Marcus J. Borg and John Dominic Crossan helpful

---

[11] 1956-58; Associate Minister, First Congregational Church, Saginaw, Michigan, 1958–1962, Organizing Minister and Minister, Westlake Presbyterian Church, Battle Creek, Michigan, 1962-1967, Minister, First Presbyterian Church, Baldwinsville, New York.

[12] Albert Schweitzer. *The Quest of the Historical Jesus: A Critical Study of Its Progress from Reimarus to Wrede* (New York: Macmillan, 1961. First German edition, 1906).

[13] Robert W. Funk, Roy W. Hoover, and The Jesus Seminar, *The Five Gospels: What Did Jesus Really Say?* (New York: Macmillan, Polebridge Press, 1993). Robert W. Funk and the Jesus Seminar. *The Acts of Jesus: What Did Jesus Really Do?* (San Francisco: Harper San Francisco, Polebridge Press, 1998). (The *Jesus Seminar* is sponsored by the Westar Institute, a scholarly think tank. It consists of some 74 New Testament scholars who have banded together with the avowed purpose of attempting to determine the authentic words and actions of Jesus.)

in the ongoing search for authenticity in the quest of the historical Jesus.[14] Lastly, I find the writings of John Spong to be extremely relevant for modern Christian theological thought.[15]

But the truth will out. For me, the truth is that there is no God up there or out there eagerly waiting to intervene in the affairs and activities of humankind. The truth for me is that humankind is totally and completely on its own. We are here. We are the meaning makers. We are the ones who fend for ourselves and define our own existence and have no outside force either to blame or to appeal.

What do I call myself today? How do I label myself? I am an existential humanist with a strong belief in evolution. I am a thorough-going agnostic as well as a committed nontheist and a *negative* atheist. In terms of any formal identification with a community of like-minded folks, I identify myself as a Unitarian-Universalist, because that is where I find many kindred spirits with open, questing minds in the search for truth.[16]

Ever since leaving the Christian ministry, I have labeled myself an apostate. I do not know if there are others who have experienced similar things. I presume there are. I believe, even though I am in the eighth decade of my life, that I am still giving birth to myself. I am still learning and growing. I am more curious than ever before. I remain thirsty for new words, new books, new thoughts, new adventures. I no longer speak of God in any traditional sense. Life for me without God has far more depth of meaning and purpose and significantly fewer stumbling blocks than I had ever experienced when I was a believer. Cheers!

---

[14] Marcus J. Borg, *Meeting Jesus Again for the First Time* (San Francisco: Harper SanFrancisco, 1994). John Dominic Crossan, *Jesus: A Revolutionary Biography* (San Francisco: Harper SanFrancisco, 1994).

[15] John Shelby Spong, *Rescuing the Bible from Fundamentalism* (San Francisco: Harper SanFrancisco, 1991) and John Shelby Spong, *Why Christianity Must Change Or Die* (San Francisco: Harper SanFrancisco, 1998).

[16] Unitarian-Universalists first identified themselves as being Christians who did not share a belief in the Trinity, i.e., God the Father, God the Son, and God the Holy Spirit. Hence the word *Unitarian* as opposed to *Trinitarian*. In the last two decades of the twentieth century, many Unitarians departed from the single godhead brand of theism to a community of free-thinkers who were skeptical of all Christian dogma and for the most part agnostic about any kind of revealed theology. Today, Unitarian-Universalists include deists, theists, Buddhists, pagans, humanists, and spiritualists of all stripes and descriptions. Some adhere to a natural theology. All adhere to the prime principle of free thought and a continuing quest for truth.

Appendix II

The Flipside of Godspeak for Non-Theists

The Flipside of Godspeak is:

saying goodbye to childhood.

ceasing to believe in fairy tales.

forsaking myths and illusions.

having a conscience and will free of the supernatural.

living without idols.

growing up.

The Flipside of Godspeak is:

holding the conviction that we are completely on our own.

taking complete and total responsibility for oneself.

accepting and bearing one's own burdens.

saying 'yes' to life on life's terms.

having the courage to take the road less traveled.

Appendix II

The Flipside of Godspeak is:

daring to look at our own constructed realities.

daring to examine the myths we have assimilated.

daring to create new accommodations.

The Flipside of Godspeak is:

giving meaning to our own existence.

giving birth to one's self.

openness to life without the dictates of irrational authority.

respect for rational authority based on significant evidence.

faith based on a preponderance of significant evidence.

The Flipside of Godspeak is:

being open to the ongoing quest for truth.

being open to what we do and do not know.

being open to new discoveries and hypotheses.

being open to truth in all fields of inquiry.

being open to the scientific method in the search for truth.

The Flipside of Godspeak is:

weighing human behavior in terms of truth.

weighing human behavior in terms of integrity.

weighing human behavior in terms of goodness.

weighing human behavior in terms of compassion.

weighing human behavior in terms of generosity.

weighing human behavior in terms of justice.

weighing human behavior in terms of respect.

weighing human behavior in terms of equity and equality.

The Flipside of Godspeak is:

basing one's values on human well-being.

basing one's behavior on human welfare.

basing one's commitments on human enrichment.

The Flipside of Godspeak is:

accepting differences within a framework of respect.

celebrating human diversity and individualism.

treating others as ends, never as means.

The Flipside of Godspeak is:

acceptance of the premise that we are the ultimate problem.

acceptance of the premise that we are the ultimate solution.

The Flipside of Godspeak is:

commitment to work unceasingly for just causes.

commitment to end deprivation for all people.

commitment to restore ravaged environments.

commitment to respect the worldwide habitat.

The Flipside of Godspeak is:

realizing that person power alone can change the world.

reserving judgment until all facts are considered.

renouncing the 'God of war' in all its manifestations.

committing to international agencies of world government.

humankind authoring the codes under which all nations live.

practicing the art of political and economic reconciliation.

The Flipside of Godspeak is:

doing love instead of talking faith.

building bridges instead of defending dogmas.

living in the here and now.

living by the best and most noble of what we know.

having respect and reverence for life in all its manifestations.

The Flipside of Godspeak is:

stewardship of the gift of life.

humility in the presence of mystery.

a sense of awe and wonder.

joy and challenge each new day until our journey's end.

Glossary

Accommodation: In Piaget, when new information clashes or is in conflict with previously assimilated information, the human organism is challenged to create a synthesis whereby the new information corrects, supplants, or otherwise provides a way to resolve the conflict.

Agnosticism: (As opposed to skepticism.) From the Greek *a* (without) and *gnosis* (knowledge). A system of belief wherein an alleged proposition or eternal truth is claimed to be unknowable. Essentially, an agnostic claims to be without valid knowledge, especially about the nature of ultimate reality and the existence of God or a god.

Apostate: One who has abandoned the faith. A person who renounces what she or he previously believed.

Assimilation: In Piaget, the absorption, internalizing, or taking into oneself various kinds of information about life, the world, and the self.

Atheist: From the Greek, *a* (without) and *theos* (god). A person who either does not believe in God, a weak or negative atheist; or a person who believes there is no God, a strong or positive atheist.

Constructivism: A name given to the philosophical/psychological belief referring to the inability of the human organism to know or to perceive reality in any direct manner. Consequently, what one believes to be reality is an invention, a creation, or a construct of the human mind. Constructivists do not deny reality. However, they deny that reality can ever be known directly. All knowledge comes to us indirectly through the interaction of our biophysical systems, our sensory perceptions, and our mental reasoning, as these processes combine to make sense of our personal life experiences. The end result is the creation of mental constructs that then become one's personal realities.

Coherence Theory of Truth: Truth is the result of the congruence of two or more propositions or hypotheses representing diverse, yet related areas of inquiry. When independent research yields hypotheses that tend to embrace the validity of the same conclusion, it is said that the several hypotheses cohere, and that this coherence is indicative of truth.

Consensus Theory of Truth: Truth is the result of significant agreement among witnesses, participants, or judges. Hence, if an impressive majority of people believe in the existence of God, then it must be true that there is such a being. If an impressive majority of people believe in heaven or hell, then it must be so.

Correspondence Theory of Truth: Truth is the result of an agreement between the alleged "facts" of a situation or proposition and the observed reality. In this manner of reasoning, whatever interpretation fits or corresponds most adequately with the alleged facts of any given situation is deemed the truth.

Deism: (As opposed to theism.) The belief that there exists an impersonal, transcendent, ultimate force or prime cause that created the cosmos and its inherent potential for growth and continued existence, but without any involvement by this force with human affairs or history. The creative force or deity is said to be transcendent but not immanent.

Epistemology: The study of various theories of knowledge or of knowledge per se. The study of how we know what we think we know. How do we know the method by which we attain knowledge is valid, and how do we know it yields truth?

Equilibration: In Piaget, when accommodation with previously assimilated information or situations is successful, the resolution constitutes a new state of equilibration, balance or harmony.

Eudaemonism: Literally, a good demon. This term indicates well-being, whether of an individual or a collective. An ethic of well-being serves to create and maintain a sense of altruistic reciprocity among individuals and collectives. Eudaemonism implies wholeness, soundness, health, and authenticity.

Existentialism: The existence of life precedes the meaning and purpose one may choose to give to that life. Existence precedes essence or meaning. First, we exist; then, we are faced with the challenge of assuming or not assuming responsibility for ourselves and the definition we give to our own existence. (This term is in opposition to the belief that there is a pre-given meaning to one's life, i.e., that meaning or essence precedes existence.)

First-Order Truth: (As opposed to second-order truth.) As used here, first-order truth is personal truth. It is an individual's claim that his/her beliefs are true. In this sense, what an individual believes reflects that person's outlook upon life and so becomes that person's personal truth as well as that person's constructed reality.

Hermeneutic: An interpretation or methodology of interpretation, often applied to principles and methods of interpreting scripture, sacred texts, and literature.

Higher Criticism: (As opposed to lower, or textual, criticism.) Higher, or historical, criticism applies to works in classical literature, art, and scripture. The art of criticism involves evaluation and analysis. The focus of higher criticism in the literary mode is upon authorship, dating of the original writing, the intended audience of the writer, the purpose of the writing, and even the site of the original writing.

Hypothesis: In the scientific method, a hypothesis is a formal statement of an assumed relationship between two or more variables stated in the form of a hypothetical proposition. Hypotheses are tested by using a null form, i.e., a hypothetical proposition stated in the negative. The purpose of research is to establish evidence that will enable the researcher to reject the null hypothesis, thus enabling the formal positive proposition to stand. Several related hypotheses that withstand challenges to the null may then be combined into a theory.

Immanent: (As opposed to transcendent.) Inherent, intrinsic, indwelling. In theology, a term that refers to a deity present and active within the affairs of human beings, communities, and nations.

Intuition: A method claiming to arrive at truth by virtue of personal experience. Intuition is outside the process of rational logic, inference, or thought. It is claiming to know by perception or immediate awareness, such as an immediate flash of insight.

Glossary

Logotherapy: The school of psychotherapy named and practiced by Viktor Frankl. Logotherapy derives from Frankl's emphasis on the importance of creating and finding meaning (logos) in one's life.

Lower Criticism: (As opposed to higher, or historical, criticism.) Lower, or textual, criticism is a form of scholarship focusing on the texts of classical literature and scripture by rigorous examination in the light of grammar, etymology, syntax, vocabulary, phrasing, style, spelling, and sentence construction. Textual criticism may contribute to the answers to questions raised by the higher criticism, especially concerning authorship and dating.

Natural Theology: (As opposed to revealed theology.) Theological study and reasoning based on observation and study of the microcosm and macrocosm of the universe. Natural theology concerns itself with inference and deduction from the observed order of the "natural" world rather than divine or supernatural revelations purported to be true and authentic.

Non-theist: From Latin *non* (no or negative), and *theos* (god). A person who rejects theism and therefore does not believe in God or gods.

Pantheism: The belief that God *is* all. Since God is all, then God is everywhere, and there is no distinction between creator and creation.

Panentheism: God is *in* all. God and the world are *not* identical. Nevertheless, all creation shares in the being of God.

Pragmatism: A theory of truth claiming that whatever works, whatever is useful, and whatever leads to solutions constitutes truth.

Prepotent: When any human need, be it psychological, physiological, mental, or spiritual, asserts itself to the point that it demands to be addressed prior to any other need, it is said to be prepotent over all other needs

Revealed Theology: (As opposed to natural theology.) Knowledge about God is the direct result of God making itself known to humanity. Revealed theology claims that humankind can only know God if and when God chooses to reveal itself. Hence, divine or supernatural self-revelation of the deity.

Scientific Method: A research methodology primarily associated with hypothesis-testing and theory-building. Results of scientific investigation are considered as approximating truth until or unless further research indicates otherwise. Propositions and hypotheses must be testable if scientific methodology is to be applied.

Second-Order Truth: (As opposed to first-order truth.) The ultimate truth about reality and the origin of the universe, the macrocosm, and the microcosm. Second-order truth *is* reality and is therefore unknowable in any final or ultimate sense.

Skepticism: (As opposed to agnosticism.) To be skeptical or to be a skeptic is to doubt, to have serious reservations about the reliability, validity, and authenticity of a belief, a tenet of faith, a reputed event, or a proposition.

Solipsism: The belief that the human mind constitutes the totality of reality. Solipsism claims there is no reality outside the mind.

Teleology: From Greek *telos* (an end). The belief that there is an end, goal, or purpose in life and the natural order. The teleological argument for the existence of God is the argument from the alleged design and purpose of nature and the universe.

Theism: (As opposed to deism.) The belief that the deity is both the transcendent creator of the universe and actively involved in the affairs of individuals, communities, and nations. Theists believe that individuals can have immediate knowledge of the deity and personal relationship with the deity via the communion of prayer and meditation.

Theory: The result of hypothesis testing and the coherence of research endeavors. A theory is a congruence of general principles arrived at via hypothesis testing, which then may be used to explain the relationship between variables and phenomena of diverse kinds.

Transcendent: (As opposed to immanent.) Referring to a deistic or theistic force that creates and maintains the universe, the macrocosm, and the microcosm. Deists claim that God is transcendent but not immanent. Theists claim that God is both transcendent and immanent.

Bibliography

Armstrong, Karen. *A History of God: The 4000 Year Quest of Judaism, Christianity and Islam*. New York: Alfred A. Knopf, 1994

Atheism Web. www.infidels.org/news/atheism.

Becker, Ernest. *The Denial of Death*. New York: The Free Press, 1973.

Bennett, Jonathan. "Glimpses of Spinoza." *The Syracuse Scholar* (Spring 1983) 43-56.

Borg, Marcus J. *Meeting Jesus Again for the First Time*. San Francisco: Harper SanFrancisco, 1994.

Bowen, Murray. *Family Therapy in Clinical Practice*. New York: Jason Aronson, 1978.

Colman, Andrew M. *Oxford Dictionary of Psychology*. Oxford: Oxford University Press, 2001.

Chasin, Richard, et al. *One Couple: Four Realities*. New York: The Guilford Press, 1990.

Crosby, John F. *Illusion and Disillusion: The Self in Love and Marriage*. Belmont, Calif: Wadsworth Publishing Company, 4th ed., 1991.

_____. *Sexual Autonomy: Toward a Humanistic Ethic*. Springfield, Ill: Charles C. Thomas, 1991.

_____. "Theories of Anxiety: A Theoretical Perspective." *The American Journal of Psychoanalysis* 36, 3 (1976).

Crossan, John Dominic. *Jesus: A Revolutionary Biography*. San Francisco: Harper SanFrancisco, 1994.

Bibliography

Crosser, Sandra. "Emerging Morality: How Children Think About Right and Wrong." Excelligence Learning Corporation. http://www.earlychildhood.com/articles/index.cfm?.

Dawkins, Richard. *The Blind Watchmaker*. New York: Ballantine, 1996.

_____. *The Selfish Gene*. New York: Oxford University Press, 1976.

Ehlert, Carl. "The Search For Truth," (sermon delivered at the Unitarian-Universalist Church of Danville, Ind. Feb. 19, 2006).

Forrester, Heinz von. "On Constructing A Reality." In *The Invented Reality*, edited by Paul Watzlawick, 41-61. New York: W. W. Norton, 1984.

Fosnot, Catherine Twomey. *Constructivism: Theory, Perspectives, and Practice*. New York: Teachers College Press, 2005.

Freud, Sigmund. *The Future of An Illusion*. New York: Anchor Books, Doubleday and Company, 1927)

Fromm, Erich. *The Art of Loving*. New York: Harper & Row, 1956.

_____. *Escape From Freedom*. New York: Holt, Rinehart and Winston, 1941.

_____. *Man For Himself*. New York: Holt, Rinehart and Winston, 1947.

_____. *Psychoanalysis And Religion*. New Haven: Yale University Press, 1950.

_____. *You Shall Be As Gods*. New York: Holt, Rinehart and Winston, 1966.

Frankl, Viktor E. *Man's Search For Meaning*. New York: Simon & Schuster, 1959

Funk, Robert W., Roy W. Hoover, and the Jesus Seminar. *The Five Gospels: What Did Jesus Really Say?* New York: Macmillan, Polebridge Press, 1993).

Funk, Robert W., and the Jesus Seminar. *The Acts of Jesus: What Did Jesus Really Do?* San Francisco: Harper SanFrancisco, Polebridge Press, 1998.

Gehman, Henry Snyder. *The New Westminster Dictionary of the Bible*. Philadelphia: Westminster Press, 1970

Gilligan, Carol. *In a Different Voice: Psychological Theory and Women's Development*. Cambridge, Mass.: Harvard University Press, 1982.

Glasersfeld, Ernst von. "An Introduction to Radical Constructivism," In *The Invented Reality*, edited by Paul Watzlawick, 17-40. New York: W.W. Norton and Company, 1984.

Bibliography

_____. "Homage To Jean Piaget (1896-1980)." *Irish Journal of Psycholgy* 18 (3), (1997) 293-306.

_____. "Introduction: Aspects of Constructivism." In *Constructivism: Theory, Perspectives, and Practice*, edited by Catherine Twomey Fosnot, 3-7. New York: Teachers College Press, 2005

_____. *Radical Constructivism: A Way of Knowing and Learning.* London: Falmer Press, 1995.

Harris, Sam. *The End of Faith: Religion, Terror, and the Future of Reason.* New York: W. W. Norton, 2004.

Joachim, Harold H. *Aristotle: The Nicomachean Ethics.* New York: Oxford University Press, 1998.

Jones, W. T. *A History of Western Philosophy.* New York: Harcourt, Brace and Company, 1952.

Kerr, Michael E., and Murray Bowen. *Family Evaluation: An Approach Based on Bowen Theory.* New York: W. W. Norton, 1988.

Keeney, Bradford P. *Aesthetics of Change.* New York: The Guilford Press, 1983.

Kohlberg, Lawrence. *The Philosophy of Moral Development.* New York: Harper & Row, 1981

Kuhn, Thomas S. *The Structure of Scientific Revolutions.* Chicago: The University of Chicago Press, 1962.

Leill, Scott M. "Shaking the Foundation of Faith." The New York Times, Nov. 18, 2005.

Leslie, Gerald, *The Family In Social Context.* 5th ed. New York: Oxford University Press, 1982.

Lloyd, Peter B. "What Is Truth?" http://easyweb.easynet.co.uk/~ursaphilos/cert04.htm.

Marian, David. "The Correspondence Theory of Truth," *The Stanford Encyclopedia of Philosophy.* Summer 2002.

Maslow, Abraham. "A Theory of Human Motivation." *Psychological Review* 50 (1943) 370-396.

May, Rollo. *Man's Search for Himself.* New York: W. W. Norton, 1953.

Merriam-Webster's Collegiate Dictionary, 11th ed., Springfield, Mass.: 2003.

Bibliography

Niebuhr, Reinhold. *Moral Man and Immoral Society: A Study of Ethics and Politics.* New York: Charles Scribner's Sons, 1932.

Paine, Thomas. *The Crisis.* Dec. 23, 1776. New York: Penguin Books, 1995.

Piaget, Jean. *Science of Education and the Psychology of the Child.* New York: Viking Press, 1971.

Randall, John Herman Jr., and Justus Buchler. *Philosophy: An Introduction.* New York: Barnes and Noble, 1942.

Sagan, Carl. *The Demon Haunted World.* New York: Ballantine, 1996.

Schweitzer, Albert. *The Quest of the Historical Jesus: A Critical Study of Its Progress From Reimarus to Wrede.* New York: Macmillan, 1961. (First German edition, 1906)

Simon, Fritz B. et al. *The Language of Family Therapy: A Systemic Vocabulary and Sourcebook.* New York: Family Process Press, 1985

Spong, John Shelby. *Rescuing the Bible From Fundamentalism.* San Francisco: Harper SanFrancisco, 1991.

_____. *Why Christianity Must Change Or Die.* San Francisco: Harper SanFrancisco, 1998.

Stein, Gordon. *An Anthology of Atheism and Rationalism.* Amherst, N.Y.: Prometheus, 1980.

Stewart, R. B. Jr. *On The Origin of Gods.* Powell, Tenn.: Powell Publishing, 2004.

Stolzenberg, Gabriel, "Can an Inquiry into the Foundations of Mathematics Tell Us Anything Interesting About Mind?" In *The Invented Reality*, edited by Paul Watzlawick, 257-308. New York: W. W. Norton, 1984.

Tillich, Paul. *The Courage To Be.* New Haven: Yale University Press, 1952.

Titus, Harold H. *Ethics For Today.* 5th ed. Belmont, Calif: Wadsworth Bublishing Company, 1973.

Watzlawick, Paul. *The Invented Reality.* New York: W. W. Norton, 1984.

_____. *Ultra-Solutions: How to Fail Most Successfully.* New York: W. W. Norton, 1988.

Weatherhead, Leslie D. *The Will of God.* New York: Abingdon Press, 1944.

Bibliography

Webster's New World Dictionary, Third College Edition. New York: Simon & Schuster, 1988.

Weeks, Gerald R. and Luciano L'Abate. *Paradoxical Psychotherapy.* New York: Bruner/Mazel, 1982.

Young, James O. "The Coherence Theory of Truth." *The Stanford Encyclopedia of Philosophy.* Summer, 2001.